THE CHARLES ATLAS STORY

THE CHARLES ATLAS STORY

The Charles Atlas Story

By
Birch Tree Publishing
Published by Birch Tree Publishing

The Charles Atlas Story
All right reserved
No part of this book may be reproduced, scanned, or distributed in any printed or electronic form without permission of Birch Tree Publishing.

2020 Copyright Birch Tree Publishing
ISBN-978-1-990089-06-0

Birch Tree Publishing

THE CHARLES ATLAS STORY

DAVID BAINES

Birch Tree Publishing

~ CHAPTER LISTING ~

Introduction — **06**

Chapter 1: In The Beginning — **07**

Chapter 2: The Mouse That Roared — **15**

Chapter 3: The Hero Of The Beach — **20**

Chapter 4: From Greek God to "Perfectly Developed" — **30**

Chapter 5: Mail Order Muscles — **47**

Chapter 6: Atlas Vs Hoffman — **68**

Chapter 7: Atlas At War — **77**

Chapter 8: Post War Muscles — **90**

Chapter 9: Evolution of a Strongman — **101**

Chapter 10: The Atlas Legacy — **106**

Introduction by David Baines

Few people in the history of the world have inspired more people to become better human beings than the legendary Charles Atlas. In this biography, I have attempted to reveal a little more of the intensely private man who literally became a living trademark. Although he was a popular and instantly recognizable public figure to five generations of Americans, the private Charles Atlas remains almost completely unknown outside the few surviving family members today.

Indeed, as the number of people who actually knew him on a personal level continues to dwindle, it is now perhaps time to put some of those fond memories and recollections of Charles Atlas on paper before the very essence of the man himself becomes lost forever. Although Atlas passed away in December 1972 at the age of 80, countless articles have appeared in magazines and on Internet websites, a testament to his enduring influence and fame in the world of bodybuilding. Most have been inaccurate and even defamatory, but none have come close to providing a glimpse into this single-minded personality beyond the public figure from those memorable comic books ads.

So here it is my tribute to Charles Atlas, a man who fought his way from obscurity and against all the odds, to reach the very pinnacle of world fame; a self-made man in every sense who pursued the American dream and lived it to the full while inspiring millions of young and not-so-young men around the world to be the very best they could be in life. And he is still inspiring young and not-so-young men today almost fifty years after his passing.

Yours in Strength and Power
David Baines

In The Beginning.....

On October 30th, 1892, in the town of Acri, Calabria, southern Italy, a Healthy baby boy called Angelo was born to Santos Siciliano and his wife Francis. He was their second son, they were a typical farming family of that area, respectable, hardworking and religious. Less than a decade later, the Siciliano family decided to spread their wings and settle in a vast and wealthy country that was promoted the world over as the land of the free and the home of the brave; the United States of America. We do not know today what prompted the Siciliano family to emigrate, but like tens of thousands of immigrants from Italy, Ireland and East Europe, the promise of a better life with new opportunities for all would have been hard to resist. Perhaps the tragic death of Vincent, their first son at the age of five years, and the reassurance of help to settle in America from relatives who were already living there might have prompted the family to leave their heartbreak, their farm, and their country, far behind.

On September 11th, 1903, the Steam Ship Roma arrived from Naples and dropped anchor just off New York City harbor. The Siciliano family, along with most other new immigrants, were transported from the pier by ferry or barge to Ellis Island where they underwent a medical inspection and document processing, which took from three to five hours to complete. Finally, they stepped onto American soil under the perpetual gaze of the statue of Liberty to begin their American dream.

The bustling streets of Brooklyn and packed tenement buildings must have been a culture shock to newly arrived immigrants. To an 11-year-old Italian immigrant who couldn't speak a word of English, Young Angelo must have yearned for the green fields and lush pastures of southern Italy where he enjoyed a carefree and happy childhood.

Contrary to popular belief, the young Italian immigrant who would later become known to the world as Charles Atlas, did not start out in life as a frail, stick thin child as was generally believed. He would later write in the November 1921 edition of physical Culture Magazine, that he was;

"......never sickly, but on the contrary rather strong, but not unusually so."

The S.S. Roma, the ship that delivered the Siciliano family to Ellis Island, New York in 1903

From 1901 to 1914, five million immigrant passed through Ellis Island.*

*It is estimated about 12 million immigrants passed through Ellis Island during the time of its operation, from 1892 to 1954. Many of them were from Southern and Eastern Europe.

01 In The Beginning

However, the unfamiliar, mean streets of Brooklyn, filled with Italian, Irish and Jewish immigrants, became a nightmare for Angelo. His unhappiness was compounded by the fact that his father, who was flatly unimpressed with his new surroundings, returned alone to Italy where he continued to farm. Angelo and his mother struggled on, living with an uncle. Angelo's mother reverted to her maiden name of Palomeni (as recorded in a 1940 US Government census), and worked as a seamstress. Angelo attended the Italian Settlement Housel to learn English, and became a frequent target for local Bullies. He was picked on almost daily unless he had a friend to walk home with after school. Eventually, he lost interest in his schoolwork, and became so weak and thin he could barely climb the steps to the family's first floor apartment on Front Street. Worse still, he suffered from frequent nose bleeds, and his mother and his family doctor were worried that Angelo was fast on his way to becoming an invalid. Today, we now recognize these traumatic symptoms and the devastating psychological effects on children and teenagers who are of victims of violence, abuse and bullying. And unlike today, Angelo did not have access to counseling and support from mental health professionals. But he still held on to his determination to overcome his limitations and become a success in life.

Little Italy, New York City, 1905. It was a neighborhood like this where young Angelo Siciliano was raised. Like most immigrant families, the Sicilianos worked hard to make ends meet, but getting ahead was an endless struggle, compounded by the discrimination against newcomers to the country at that time.

01 In the Beginning

Angelo Siciliano aged 11 years in 1903, shortly after arriving in the United States.

11/In the Beginning

Before Angelo's formal education ended in 1908 at the age of 16, he participated on a day trip to the Brooklyn Museum with the Italian Settlement House, established by the Reverend William E. Davenport. As fate would have it, this was a field trip that would change Angelo's life forever. As the rest of the group eagerly fanned out in the museum to take in the exhibits, Angelo's eye locked onto a stone statue of the Greek hero, Hercules. He was transfixed by the powerful muscles of the figure, which was placed alongside other famous statues such as the dying gladiator, the wrestlers, and the discus thrower. The perfect physiques of the figures forever captured in marble deeply impressed Anglo, who asked Mr. Davenport if such perfectly developed men really existed?
"How did they get those muscles? They look kinda fishy to me", he mused.

The kindly reverend, an educated man, regaled Angelo with stories about Milo of Crotona and how he developed his strength, and how the ancient Greeks worshipped well-developed athletes who were rewarded with crowns of laurel leafs and held in high regard.
"Do you think I can develop myself into being like one of these men?" Asked Angelo.
"Almost anybody can be strong. Anyone who is willing to work for it can obtain the same muscular development," replied Davenport. Seeing Angelo's determination to build a muscular body, Davenport directed him to the local YMCA, which had a well-equipped gymnasium and experienced instructors on hand to offer instruction.

But Angelo was too poor to pay the membership fee and had to satisfy himself by watching how some exercises were performed, then copy them at home. In his room, he managed to construct a makeshift pulley exerciser, and fashioned a homemade barbell using a broom handle and two rocks.
He pasted a picture of Eugen Sandow, the famous Prussian strongman on his dresser for inspiration, and began to exercise every day in the hope of transforming himself into a living embodiment of Hercules or Apollo.

01 In the Beginning

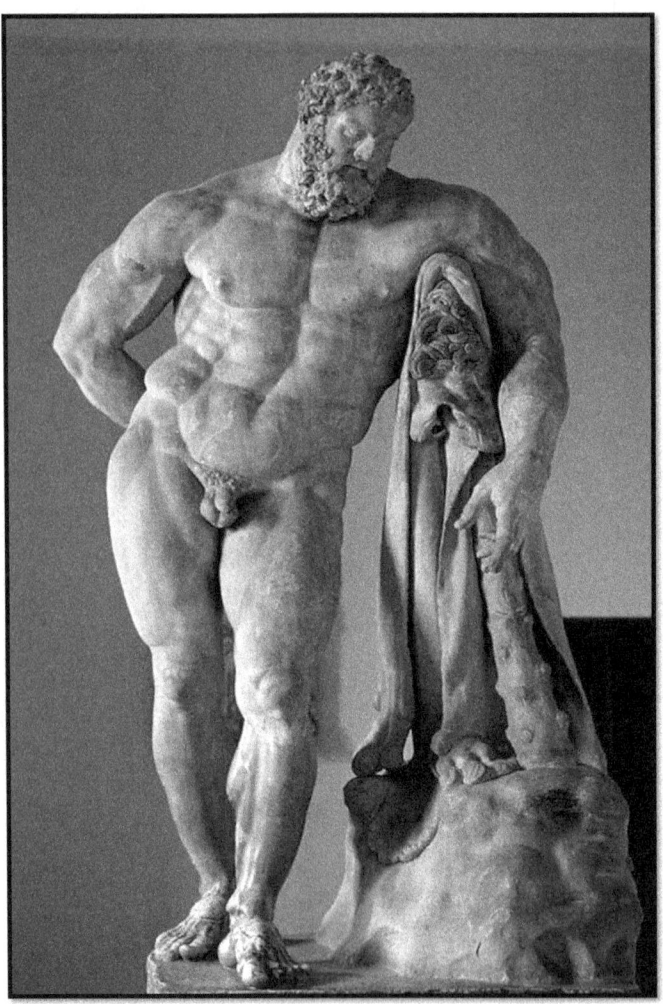

A statue of Hercules similar to the one that sparked young Angelo's single-minded determination to build a powerful, muscular body that would win respect and admiration

01 In the Beginning

During the summer of 1908, Angelo, who had by this time adopted the nickname "Charlie," took a pretty girl to the beach. While they were sitting on the sand, chatting and enjoying the view, a brawny lifeguard spotted the girl and wondered why she was keeping the company of an unremarkable looking, pale, still-stick thin teenager. The bully, who was supposed to be a life saver, decided to become a heartbreaker. He walked up to Charlie, ridiculed him, kicked sand in his face and invited the girl to spend the day with him. The girl accepted and walked off with the bully, leaving Charlie alone and humiliated.

Tobacco smoking adolescent "toughs" like these sold newspapers on the streets of New York City, and picked fights with less formidable young boys like Angelo Siciliano.

01 In the Beginning

To help make ends meet at home, Charlie found employment in a leather factory that produced ladies pocket books. The superintendent, Mr. Welch, was impressed with the young man's skill and artistic abilities and placed him over his fellow workers. To stop the grumbling and resentment over Charlie's promotion, the towering Welch, who stood 6ft 10in tall, picked up a wooden stool and threatened to smash it over the head of anyone who bothered his young Italian protégé. Needless to say there were no complaints after that.

The work gave Charlie enough pocket money to buy Physical Culture magazine, published by the eccentric health & fitness guru, Bernarr MacFadden, who pioneered the physical culture industry in America and became a pivotal figure in the young immigrant's future success. As Charlie recalled much later in his life, he was probably "more interested in muscles than any kid who ever lived."

02 The Mouse that Roared

One Halloween night when walking home from work, Charlie was jumped by a thug who dragged him into a dark alley. The antagonist, a well-known local bully, beat Charlie into unconsciousness with a sock filled with ashes for no reason other than he was an easy target. After regaining consciousness, Charlie rested up for a while in the alley before painfully making his way home, bloodied and bruised. If he was thinking that he would find comfort and safety in the family apartment, he was tragically mistaken.
His uncle, looking over the beaten and disheveled youth said; "what's the idea getting into fights?" Then gave Charlie another beating.

That night, Charlie wept hot bitter tears. He vowed in prayer before God that he would never let another man touch him again. Yet his best efforts to develop a mighty physique with his home-made equipment had amounted to naught. There had to be a way he mused, but how? He was tired of being picked on by the neighborhood bullies when he didn't have a friend to accompany him home from school. One weekend in 1909, Charlie visited the Brooklyn Zoo. He needed to get away from everything and think.

Standing before a lion cage, he watched as the big cat yawned, then stretched and tensed its powerful muscles, which ran around its body "like rabbits running around under a rug," he would later recall. Then a light bulb went on inside Charlie's head. How does the king of the jungle get to be so powerfully built without lifting weights?

02 The Mouse that Roared

With his brain working overtime, Charlie left the zoo, went home and dumped his home made equipment. He intensified his studies on health and fitness by reading *Physical Culture* magazine, and began to experiment with non-apparatus exercises that consisted mainly of bodyweight exercises and self-resistance movements. One day he found some scrap iron and sold it to a junkyard dealer for ten cents. With the money in one hand and a sandwich in the other, Charlie would sit through two or three acts.

Afterwards, he would closely question the strongmen on their diet, their exercise regime, and other health related questions. He was finally able to join the YMCA, where he would try out every exercise known to the instructors. Although the gymnasium was full of equipment, Charlie found that he got faster and more effective results with the non-apparatus exercises, making steady progress week by week.

As he gained in muscular size and strength, Charlie established an exercise regime that included those exercises that gave him quick results, while discarding others that he found laborious or non-productive. He particularly like the 'dip' or push up, which was particularly effective in quickly developing his chest, arms and shoulder muscles, and it became the most important exercise in the future body building course he would market.

With patience and experimentation, Charlie developed his own exercise regime into a highly potent system that packed pounds of muscle onto his slender frame and doubled his strength in less than a year. He began to look better, feel better, and slept better. He filled out his clothes so much with hard packed muscle that girls that ignored him before began to flirt with him, other boys wanted him on their sports teams, and the local neighborhood 'toughs' began to avoid him, and with good reason.

02 The Mouse that Roared

One night Charlie encountered the thug that gave him the beating of his life on Halloween night a year before, and returned the compliment. He abhorred violence, but he knew that the only way to cure a habitual bully was to give him as taste of his own medicine. From that point on, nobody picked on "Charlie" Siciliano again.

No one would dare!

02 The Mouse that Roared

The April 1907 edition of Physical Culture magazine. Angelo acquired a huge wealth of knowledge on health, fitness, diet, and exercise by studying this and other similar publications of the day. He would later model for the magazine.

02 The Mouse that Roared

By the time he was 19, Charlie began to look very much like the well proportioned Greek gods that he admired. One day at the Rockaway Beach, a friend pointed to a wooden statue of the Greek god, Atlas, atop the Atlas Hotel. Charlie liked the sound of that, and would later adopt the stage name "Atlas," which sounded much more American that his very Italian sounding surname of Siciliano.
In white, protestant, middle class America, prejudice was still very much alive against the different migrant communities.

Curley's Atlas Hotel, Rockaway Park, NY (1911) opposite Rockaway Beach, where Charlie would spend many summer days with friends.

03   HERO OF THE BEACH

One blustery afternoon at Brooklyn's Dika Beach, Charlie noticed a boat about a mile out in the sea with the occupants frantically waving a white shirt, as if to catch the attention of anyone on the beach who might see them. Without a second thought, the muscular nineteen year-old swam out to the boat only to find that the occupants had lost their oars. To avoid drifting further out to sea, Charlie tied the bow rope around his waist and towed the boat to the shore and much applause from the crowd that had gathered to watch the rescue. This heroic feat was later recorded by Robert Ripley in *'Ripley's Believe it or not!'* If the brawny lifeguard who kicked sand in Charlie's face two years before was still there, he certainly didn't have the courage to rescue the boaters himself, or try to pick on Charlie a second time!

On another occasion at Bayville, Long Island, Charlie was playing sports with a few friends when he noticed that a group of other teenagers were swimming back and forth to a floating platform anchored off shore, but one young man stayed put. Eventually, the group approached Charlie, thinking that he was the lifeguard for the beach. Their friend, they explained, had become too frightened to leave the platform and swim back, as the water had become deeper because of the tide. Even though they were all good swimmers, their friend just wouldn't budge. And besides, it was getting cooler and their friend was beginning to turn blue with the cold.
"What makes you think he'll come back with me?" demanded Charlie.
"Because you are big and strong, so he'll definitely trust you," they replied.

As Charlie was a strong swimmer and had practiced lifesaving techniques all summer long, he decided to swim out and bring the frightened youth back to shore. The young man was blue with the cold and paralyzed with fear. He resolutely refused to budge and insisted that his rescuer find a boat. Before the frightened swimmer suffered from hypothermia, Charlie decided to swim back to shore, located a row boat, and rescued the trembling swimmer. Such feats only added to his growing popularity with the local girls!

03 HERO OF THE BEACH

The teenage Angelo "Charlie" Siciliano, rescuer of weak swimmers and vanquisher of Brooklyn's street thugs.

03 HERO OF THE BEACH

Providence, it seemed, would order Charlie's footsteps in such a way that he couldn't avoid running into people that needed rescuing from dicey situations. On one such occasion, he was heading home from the YMCA gymnasium, where he spent the evening practicing wrestling and gymnastics. Indeed, by his early twenties, he had become a world-class acrobat. As he walked to the Flatbush Avenue station to take the train home, he noticed a group of men teasing a young woman. Thinking that she knew them, Charlie paid no attention to the group until the young woman called out to him, tearfully pleading with him to help her out.
After Charlie quickly determined that the young woman did not know her antagonists, he took her by the arm and led her away from the group.
"Come with me, I'll see that you get home," he assured her.

The group of lowlifes crowded around Charlie and began to threaten him. Without much effort, the muscular teen simply pushed a couple of them aside and warned them to leave him - and the girl - alone if they didn't want to get hurt. They quickly stepped aside after Charlie's brief but direct display of strength. As the couple walked away, one of them shouted a threat to 'get' Charlie the next time they saw him.

Once the young lady had been safely escorted to the station platform, Charlie returned to the hecklers:
"Here I am, if you want to get me! But curs like you wouldn't try to get a man: weak girls are your game!"
A member of the group, obviously the dumbest one with the biggest mouth, yelled back, "We'll get you yet!"
"Anytime you like! You'll find me here every night about this time. I'll Be looking out for you to get me," replied Charlie.

03 HERO OF THE BEACH

Needless to say, the girl-baiters never accepted his challenge, and probably thought twice about picking on an attractive young woman again, lest they encounter an angry Greek god a second time.

Although Charlie had not yet reached his full potential as a strength athlete, his physical fitness, stamina and strength were still something to behold. At the age of 19, he encountered a group of four men who were trying in vain to lift an automobile off the ground just high enough for the driver to slip on the spare wheel. Exhausted by their efforts, they practically collapsed on the sidewalk, seemingly unable to come up with a solution to their problem. Charlie walked up and offered to lift the vehicle for them.

"Awe, what's the matter with him?" One of them exclaimed.
Ignoring the jibe, Charlie walked up to the car, gripped the wheel arch with both hands and tensed every muscle in his body. At first nothing happened, but then, inch by inch, with every muscle fiber straining to the maximum, the automobile lifted off the ground, allowing the driver to slip the spare wheel onto the axle. The group were astonished.

"Gee, ain't he strong?" gasped a young boy from within the crowd. The rest of the group were momentarily speechless, and along with handshakes and back slapping, threw a dozen questions at Charlie concerning his physical strength and how they could get strong like him.

By the summer of 1911, Charlie needed to earn more money than his modest salary from the leather factory. He landed a temporary job of demonstrating spring exercisers, or chest expanders, in and empty store window on Broadway. He was hired along with another strongman Earle E. Liederman, by physical culturalist Abe Boshes who had won Bernarr MacFadden's 'perfectly developed man' contest in 1903. Standing a mere 5ft 3ins, Boshes was a literal pocket Hercules who was appointed by U.S. president Woodrow Wilson, to be his personal health advisor.

03 HERO OF THE BEACH

Abe Boshes, who won Bernarr McFadden's 'America's Most Perfectly Developed Man' contest in 1903. Boshes stood 5ft 3ins tall and weighed 150lbs. He was able to press 220lbs above his head with one arm, and travelled the country as a Vaudeville strongman and wrestler.

03 HERO OF THE BEACH

Charlie and Earle, who was the son of Swedish immigrants, both shared the American Dream and were determined to make the big time.
After his temporary contract with Boshes had finished, Charlie demonstrated and sold the exercisers on his own to make a little more money.
He described this as a 'happy combination', getting a workout while showing off his physique and making money all at the same time.

As fortune would have it, a professional stage Strongman by the name of Adolph Nordquest, spotted Charlie and offered him the opportunity to partner with him to perform a short…12 minute strength and hand balancing act at a popular theater on Coney Island. The show went on for several months, after which Charlie opened up his own strongman show on Coney Island's Surf Avenue, using the name 'Atlas.'

Resplendent in gladiator boots, white tights and a leopard skin leotard, the aspiring Hercules would start his act by performing a sort of muscle dance, followed by bending railroad spikes, tearing telephone books in two, lifting two men aloft, and lying on a bed of nails eating a banana while three men stood on his chest. Many years later he would recall how women used to faint when he did that. He also filled in as a part-time janitor with a reduced price on hot dogs. It was during his strong man act that Charlie met Margaret Cassano, whom He married in 1918.

Charlie also had a dedicated young fan called Joe Bonomo. The 16 year old Brooklyn native was the youngest son of Sephardic Jewish immigrants from Izmir, Turkey and was nicknamed "little Joe" because of his small thin stature. The family made and sold a popular ice cream, including hard candy and their famous Turkish Taffy. Joe would go on to become a movie stunt double and a successful businessman and promoter of health & fitness, rivaling even his hero, Charles Atlas for a time.

03 HERO OF THE BEACH

After his strongman acted ended, Charlie was approached by his friend, Earle Liederman who invited him to become part of a new stage act called the Orpheum Models. Both men were covered in white powder, giving them the appearance of living statues. Together their display of muscle control, feats of strength and hand balancing was a sensation. The act sold out all over Vaudeville for a total of 44 weeks, until Liederman decided to quit in order to market his own mail order bodybuilding course.

Atlas the Coney Island strongman (Circa 1918)

03 HERO OF THE BEACH

After his double act with Liederman was finished, Charlie decided to move on from 'the stage' and pondered on his next step. He was now married with a son, Charles junior, born in December 1918, followed by a daughter, Diane, born the following year. He made a decent living as a popular model for artists, and sculptors, and even allowed his photos to be used to promote Earle Liederman's mail order bodybuilding course, but he desired to provide his family with a secure and prosperous future: to reach for the stars and live the American dream to the full.

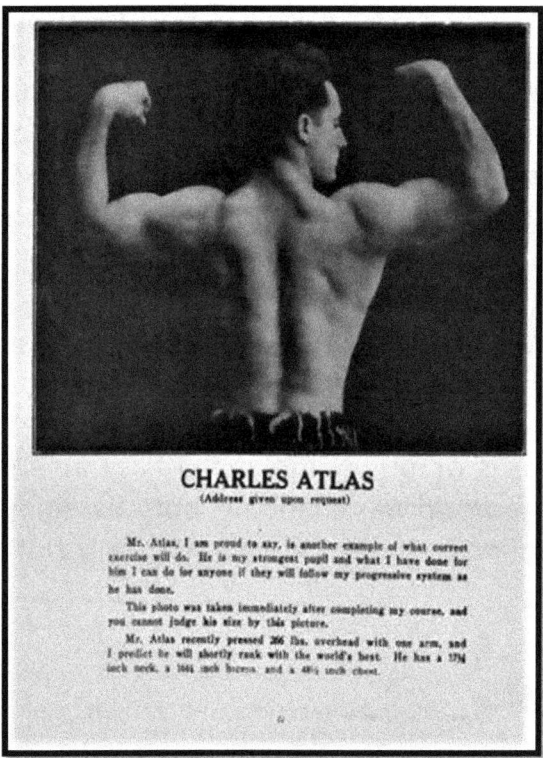

Before winning international fame as America's most perfectly developed man, Charlie helped Earle E. Liederman to sell his mail order bodybuilding course by allowing his photograph to be used in an early promotional brochure. By the time the two met in 1916, Atlas was already a powerfully built athlete and was not the product of Liederman's course. However, it was common for prominent strength athletes of the day such as Joe Bonomo, Clevio Massimo, George Jowett, and Earle E. Liederman to help one another out in this manner. Only Charles Atlas and his *Dynamic Tension* course endured throughout most of the 20th century and into the millennium, such was (and still is) his enduring fame.

03 HERO OF THE BEACH

The early 20th century was truly the golden age of the Vaudeville strong men and many earned small fortunes by performing breath-taking feats of strength that would make most 21st century bodybuilders green with envy. By far the most popular turn of the century performer, era was the Prussian strongman Eugene Sandow, who popularized exercise by opening Gymnasiums, selling exercise equipment and pioneered the use of food supplements.

He also dispensed health and diet advice to wealthy clients. In March 1911, Sandow was given the title, by royal warrant, Professor of Scientific and Physical Culture by King George V. In 1913 the English strongman, Edward Aston set a new world record in the bent arm press by raising 285 lbs above his head, at a body-weight of 170lbs. The celebrated German strongman, Arthur Saxon, who weighed 200 lbs, bettered Aston by lifting 370lbs using the same technique. However, years before these two men came on the scene, Eugene Sandow gave an astonishing demonstration of strength by lifting a platform on his shoulders that supported 19 people and a dog!

The strongman act continued on until the outbreak of the First World War, by which time music halls and Vaudeville had been largely replaced by movie theaters and night clubs. Most strongmen had, by that time, either retired, eked out a living with traveling circuses, or found employment as trainers in gymnasiums and wrestling clubs. The world was changing, but Atlas knew in his heart that his future lay in promoting his body beyond modeling, but how?

03 HERO OF THE BEACH

Contemporary strongmen of the early 20th century were (Top left) Eugen Sandow, (Top right) Edward Aston (Bottom left)

04 'PERFECTLY DEVELOPED'

In 1918, the year that Charlie married Margaret Cassano, the New York Daily News decided to hold a nationwide photo contest to find the 'modern Apollo'.
By this time, 19 year old Joe Bonomo was posing as an artist's model for a studio in Greenwich Village. He had built up a graceful but powerful physique, thanks to the valuable advice on training and nutrition given to him by Charles Atlas.

The art students decided to enter Bonomo in the modern Apollo contest without his knowledge, and sent in a few sketches of him posing as a sort of Greek god. Along with his physical measurements, name and address. Joe knew nothing about this until a letter arrived from the contest editor stating that a sketch was no good, as several photographs from each contestant was required for the judges. At first, Joe was tempted to throw the letter away, but then remembered how, like a certain young Italian immigrant, he wept and prayed to grow into a muscular Greek god.

After hunting down Charlie, Joe persuaded the popular strength athlete to help him with the photographs needed to enter the contest. Charlie admitted that he was tempted to enter the contest for himself, but decided against it as he was a strongman, not a beauty! However he went to work on Joe, loaning him his Coney Island strongman outfit, and even helped Joe to pose for the photographs.
The contest which attracted over 5,000 entries, was narrowed down to twelve finalists.

On October 30th, 1918, the twelve men appeared before a panel of artists and sculptors who picked Joe as the winner. Joe won $1,000 in prize money and a ten week movie contract, appearing in *"A Light In The Dark"*, with silent movie star Hope Hampton. This was Joe's entry into the movie world as a top Hollywood stuntman. The 'Modern Apollo' was Charlie's first successful student. In later years Joe always gave Charlie the credit for his lifelong successes as a movie stuntman, strongman, and entrepreneur.

31/ FROM GREEK GOD TO 'PERFECTLY DEVELOPED'

04 'PERFECTLY DEVELOPED'

Joe Bonomo aged 16, poses with Angelo "Charlie" Siciliano aged 25 in 1917 Plus by this time Charlie was a popular sculptor's model and all round athlete.

04 'PERFECTLY DEVELOPED'

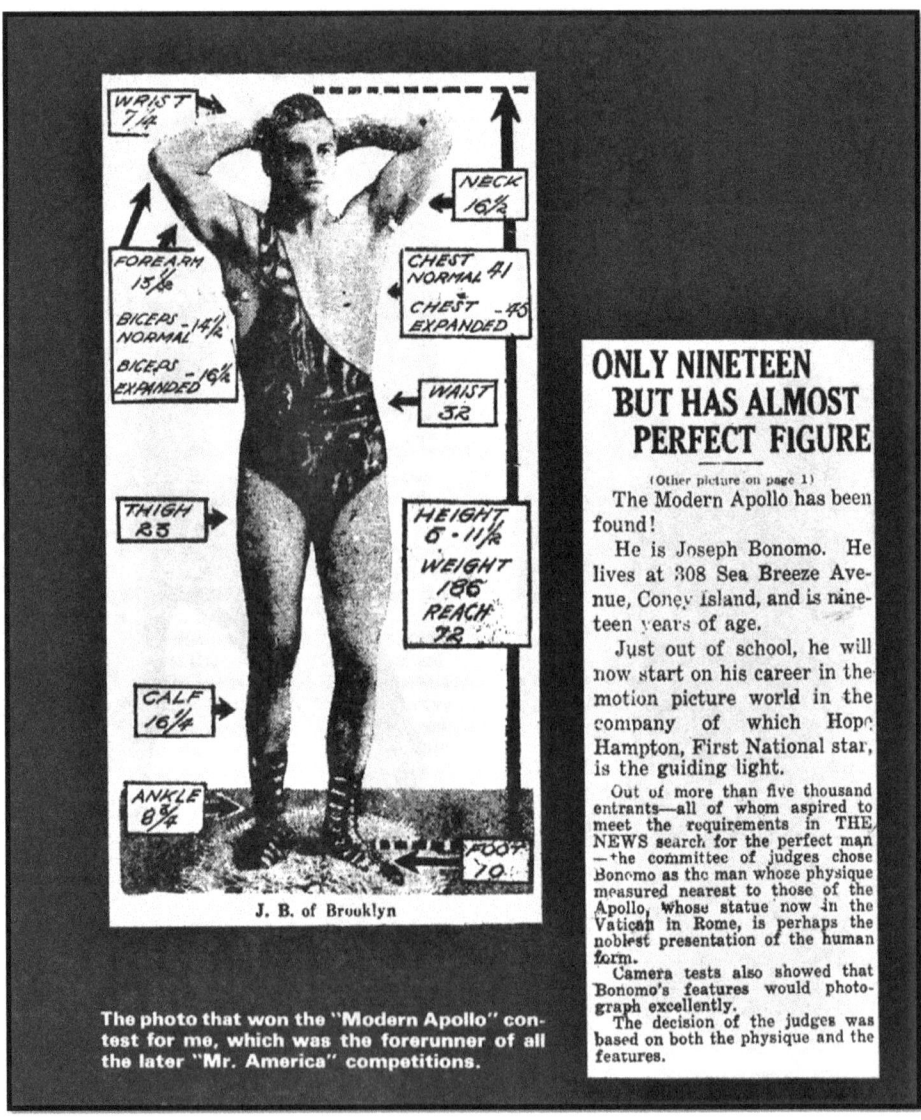

The photo that won the "Modern Apollo" contest for me, which was the forerunner of all the later "Mr. America" competitions.

ONLY NINETEEN BUT HAS ALMOST PERFECT FIGURE

(Other picture on page 1)

The Modern Apollo has been found!

He is Joseph Bonomo. He lives at 308 Sea Breeze Avenue, Coney Island, and is nineteen years of age.

Just out of school, he will now start on his career in the motion picture world in the company of which Hope Hampton, First National star, is the guiding light.

Out of more than five thousand entrants—all of whom aspired to meet the requirements in THE NEWS search for the perfect man —the committee of judges chose Bonomo as the man whose physique measured nearest to those of the Apollo, whose statue now in the Vatican in Rome, is perhaps the noblest presentation of the human form.

Camera tests also showed that Bonomo's features would photograph excellently.

The decision of the judges was based on both the physique and the features.

The "Modern Apollo" contest held by the New York Daily News in 1920 launched Joe Bonomo's silent movie career. The following year Angelo Siciliano won America's Most Handsome Man contest with his film star looks and perfect physique, setting him on the road to world-wide fame

33/ FROM GREEK GOD TO 'PERFECTLY DEVELOPED'

With his film star good looks and knockout body, Angelo "Charlie" Siciliano was practically guaranteed fame and fortune the moment he became the legendary Charles Atlas!

04 'PERFECTLY DEVELOPED'

From 1916 onward, Charlie was a popular artist and sculptor's model. Having been approached at the beach by an admiring artist who introduced him to society sculptor, Mrs. Harry Payne-Whitney. The aesthetic beauty of his physique and his ability to hold difficult poses for long periods, earned him an income of $100 per week at a time when other models were earning 50 cents an hour. He posed for over 75 statues and other works of art for Arthur Lee, Fred McMonnies, Tony Salemme, Stirling Caulder and James Earle Fraser. When he walked into a studio, people would call out 'here comes the Greek god.' One particular studio janitor baited him for two years with derogatory jibes. Finally the usually quiet and polite strongman had reached his breaking point and rounded on his antagonist;

"I've had enough of you, now I'm going to hoit you! I'm gonna send you to the hospital!"

Charlie thumped the man, and felt sick about it for two weeks afterwards. Today decades after Atlas passed away, examples of his famous physique can be seen in over 75 magnificent statues around the United States. He is Alexander Hamilton, outside the Treasury Building in Washington D.C., the Dawn of Glory Statue in Brooklyn's Prospect Park, George Washington in Washington Square Park NYC, and Civic Virtue, now located at Green –Wood Cemetery in Brooklyn, just to name but a few of them.

35/ FROM GREEK GOD TO 'PERFECTLY DEVELOPED'

04 'PERFECTLY DEVELOPED'

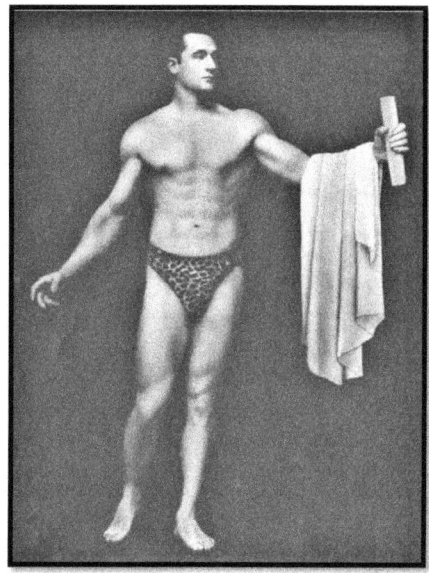

Angelo "Charlie" Siciliano, the Greek God from Brooklyn was so popular with artists and sculptors, he was paid $100 per week when most other models were paid 50 cents per hour.

04 'PERFECTLY DEVELOPED'

In 1921 Bernarr MacFadden decided to hold 'America's Most Handsome Man' contest. It was a photo contest only, and the winner would receive a cheque for $1,000 and have his photographs published in *Physical Culture* magazine. Atlas decided to enter and sent in several photos of himself clad in his leopard skin outfit. As he later recalled in an interview:

"It was tough waiting at first, said Atlas. My wife and I were pretty low on funds, for our first baby came along a little while before, and we were in debt. Three months went by and by then I had almost forgotten about the contest. But one day a telegram arrived saying that I had won. I remember running to my wife, yelling, 'Marge! We've won $1,000!' At last, after making pocketbooks for so long, I had something worth while to put in one. We paid our debts, including $50 to the photographer who had been a good sport enough to gamble on me." (The family Circle, January 20th, 1939)

Atlas continued to model for top artists and sculptors in New York City, and was used by MacFadden as a fitness model for his magazine. In October 1922, MacFadden held a second contest, this time for 'America's Most Perfectly Developed Man.' The contest was held before an audience at Madison Square Garden, and attracted over 750 contestants. One of the entrants was none other than Joe Bonomo. According to Joe in his autobiography, The Strongman (Joe Bonomo Studios Inc., 1968), he and Atlas trained together in the spirit of friendly rivalry, and even bet each other $10 on which one of the two would win the title. As Joe explained in his autobiography:

04 'PERFECTLY DEVELOPED'

"We both wanted to win for we realized what it would mean for our careers. And just for the record, I had my OWN leopard skin, so now we were starting even. The contest opened with great fanfare with entries from all over the world – many of them splendid specimens of manhood. However, when the contest had progressed through the preliminaries, Charlie and I were running neck and neck, tied for first place. We remained tied through the eliminations and the finals were set for the following Monday night. I remember that Monday all too well. Something told me not to go to work at the studio that day, but I went anyway and broke my leg crashing a motorcycle. As the judges refused to alter the title to 'The World's Most Perfectly Developed Man with a Broken leg,' Charlie not only won the title and the cash prize, but my ten dollars as well. We still kid each other about that. I claim he won by default, but Charlie says he could have broken both his legs and still have beaten me...... but it was all in fun." (The Strongman, page 48)

The title and the money gave the Brooklyn Adonis a huge boost. The first prize diploma presented to Atlas bore his name as 'Charles Siciliano Atlas', and his official Title as 'America's Most Perfectly developed Man.' Later that year, Charlie Officially changed his name to Charles Atlas, and there was little doubt among leading sculptors, artists, physical culture experts and medical doctors, that he really was the most perfectly developed man they had ever laid eyes on.
Mac Fadden agreed, and decided to cancel all future 'perfectly developed' reasoning that Atlas would win them every time.

38/ FROM GREEK GOD TO 'PERFECTLY DEVELOPED'

39/ FROM GREEK GOD TO 'PERFECTLY DEVELOPED'

Building the Physique of a "Greek God"

By Angelo Siciliano (Charles Atlas)

The Second and Concluding Instalment of the Personally Told Life Story of the Winner of PHYSICAL CULTURE's $1,000 Prize Contest for the World's Most Handsome Man

PERHAPS I may seem to be laying too much stress on the acquisition of mere strength. I don't mean to. Health is the important thing, and excepting as the development of one's muscles aids in bringing health, it doesn't amount to much. Indeed no one can acquire great strength unless his health be good.

Of course no one can read PHYSICAL CULTURE, as I did, without realizing that the important end of all exercise is not the incidental development of the muscles, but the acquirement of health. So I knew that while I could get big muscles without gaining health, I could not very well acquire robust health without incidentally developing my muscles, which, as a matter of fact, did not displease me.

I knew I must live right to be the robust man I aimed to be. I knew that I must avoid tobacco and liquor, of course. Every athlete and every trainer of athletes knows that. But I discovered that there were other stimulants to be avoided; stimulants that affected the heart—that most vital organ, which must be sound to enable any effort at development to come to anything. So coffee and tea had to be cut out. No doubt many persons go through life fairly well while indulging in these stimulants, but I don't hesitate to say that no one who does so indulge ever acquires the vitality that comes of what I would call clean living. I think one of the finest things that was ever said of me was that I radiated health and vitality. And from the little experience I have had I venture to say that there are very few persons in the world who cannot do the same if they will only give a few minutes a day to taking the exercises necessary, and will cut out the stimulants that only excite them to exertions they are not fit to take and which always leave them with the craving for more stimulants. As the expression goes, they inevitably soon come to live on their nerves—their whipped up nerves.

40/ FROM GREEK GOD TO 'PERFECTLY DEVELOPED'

Building the Physique of a "Greek God"

Perhaps it doesn't become a young man to seem to preach even the gospel of health, but this is my chance to say my say, and I want to do it. I am impelled to it by seeing so many weaklings wherever I go. And when I know that it is unnecessary for most of them to be what they are I think I may be excused for speaking out.

I do delight in my strength, but more than that I rejoice in a robustness of health that makes my life a joy every moment; and it is only natural that I should show it in a buoyancy of spirits that makes it seem as if I hadn't a care in the world. Of course I have cares and troubles, but the mere joy of living takes the sting out of disappointments and the heaviness out of trouble.

I am often asked which exercises are the best for development and hence for health. It isn't easy for me to prescribe for anyone else, but for myself I like best the dipping exercise and walking, though, as I have said, I go through a great many because I want to have an all-around development rather than an abnormal one in any way. But for a beginner any exercise should be taken easily—a few times at first, and increased by degrees.

One of the best exercises is wrestling. If gone at moderately at first and made strenuous gradually. You have read the story of the wrestling match between Hercules and Antaeus. Every time Antaeus was thrown to the earth by Hercules he grew stronger. Finally Hercules conquered him by squeezing him to death. Perhaps I am wrong because I am not learned, but it has always seemed to me to show the esteem the Greeks had for wrestling. At any rate, as the Greeks seemed to know more than any other people about developing the human body I have always looked on wrestling as the one best contest exercise.

I don't mean to decry boxing; it is a splendid exercise, and it is one that helps to acquire agility and poise and assurance. It is true that in ordinary life a man is seldom called on to exercise his ability with his fists, but it gives one a very pleasant sense of power. I try as much as possible to keep out of trouble, but once I was in a subway car where a party of noisy young ruffians occupied more seats than they were entitled to. I didn't care for myself; I preferred standing to getting in a row; but at one of the stations a feeble old woman got in and looked helplessly at a bench intended for three but fully filled by two sprawling toughs who didn't make the least move to let her sit down.

I couldn't stand that, so although I didn't know what

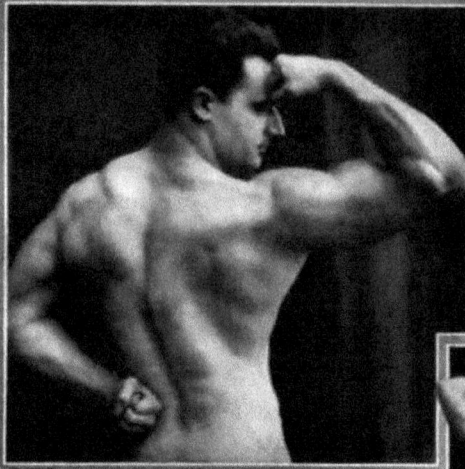

The reasons why Mr. Siciliano looks so happy is this photograph are also in the picture with him. Since it was taken, there is still another in the family.

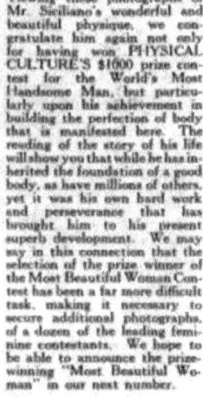

Viewing these photographs of Mr. Siciliano's wonderful and beautiful physique, we congratulate him again not only for having won PHYSICAL CULTURE'S $1000 prize contest for the World's Most Handsome Man, but particularly upon his achievement in building the perfection of body that is manifested here. The reading of the story of his life will show you that while he has inherited the foundation of a good body, as have millions of others, yet it was his own hard work and perseverance that has brought him to his present superb development. We may say in this connection that the selection of the prize winner of the Most Beautiful Woman Contest has been a far more difficult task, making it necessary to secure additional photographs of a dozen of the leading feminine contestants. We hope to be able to announce the prize-winning "Most Beautiful Woman" in our next number.

41/ FROM GREEK GOD TO 'PERFECTLY DEVELOPED'

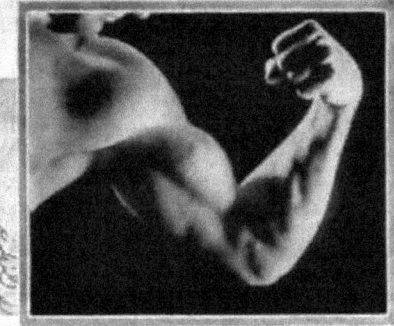

Illustrating the perfection and symmetry of Mr. Siciliano's development, you will see that there is scarcely any perceptible difference in the power and beauty of his two arms, both of which are shown here. Incidentally, the fist-bending or wrist-circling action presented, provides a vigorous exercise for the entire arm in general, and for the forearm in particular.

kind of a row I was going to let myself in for, I went over and said, "Haven't you the decency to make room for that old lady?"

"Aw! what's the matter with you?" was the only answer I received; and neither of them gave a sign of moving.

I grabbed the biggest of them by the collar and snatched him up off the seat and tossed him aside. I expected him to show fight, and for a moment it looked as if he meant to, but I guess he had realised my strength from the way I had lifted him and thrown him aside, for with no more than a muttered growl he slunk away.

Now if I hadn't been strong and hadn't known I could give a good account of myself I wouldn't have dared do that. And the old lady would have had to stand in the swaying car. Of course it made it easier that the fellow knew I had a grip of iron and could handle him without difficulty, even if I wasn't so very husky looking. I weighed then only one hundred and forty-five pounds, but I could lift a man of two hundred and four pounds and put him up over my head. That is, I not only could but had done so.

I want to say that exercises and leaving stimulants alone are not enough in themselves to bring good health. Food is an important factor. It doesn't require that one should be rich to be able to obtain the good, wholesome food that is necessary. As a matter of fact the people of wealth probably feed themselves worse than the moderately poor. They eat too much and they eat too highly spiced foods. In fact they are the ones of whom it can truly be said that they live to eat.

The amount of food required to keep a strong man in the best of condition is much less than is supposed. And the most wholesome and the most palatable food is seldom expensive; so that no one need be deterred from right living on the plea of its cost. A simple, well-balanced meal well chewed and had in cheerful company is within the means of anybody who can buy food at all. When I have eaten a full meal I like to be unconscious of the process of digestion. And I want hunger and not merely appetite to urge me to my next meal.

There is the matter of water, too. One should drink plenty of it; and one should use it freely on the outside of the body. I wish I could convince the girls I see on the street that water, inside and out, is the best cosmetic they could use. It isn't the roses on the cheeks that indicate health, though when they are natural they do make for beauty. A clear skin is more often a sign of health than even the natural roses that adorn the cheeks; and certainly the artificial roses that bloom on the faces of our girls indicate not only poor health, but poor reasoning powers. Nobody is deceived, but many are grieved.

Swimming is another good exercise, besides being a very useful accomplishment and a

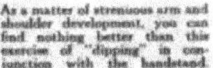

As a matter of strenuous arm and shoulder development, you can find nothing better than this exercise of "dipping" in conjunction with the handstand.

42/ FROM GREEK GOD TO 'PERFECTLY DEVELOPED'

Building the Physique of a "Greek God"

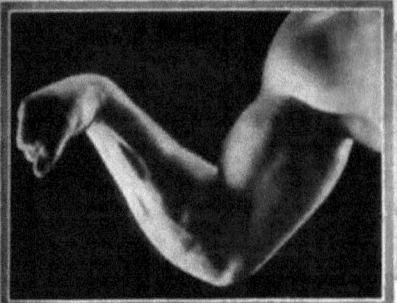

These photographs show the continuation of the wrist-circling exercise shown on the opposite page. They are extraordinary photographs of the anatomy of a perfect pair of arms.

very delightful pastime. Any one can learn to swim in a week; and if more persons did learn there would be fewer deaths from drowning. I have heard it said that it is always the good swimmers who drown. That isn't true. It is the reckless swimmers who drown; those who take risks that are unreasonable.

"The dip," usually done on the floor, is more effective and interesting performed on chairs.

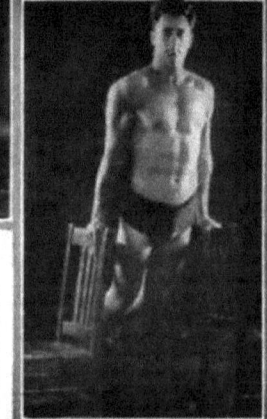

Any ordinary pair of chairs will suffice for this body-dipping exercise in which one raises and lowers the weight of the entire body. Your "resistance" in this case will depend upon how much you weigh. Place the hands on the backs of the chairs, raise and lower the body while holding the feet up. If you can do it once, it is a stunt. If you can do it ten times, it is an exercise.

And the panic that is born of fear of the water is a prolific cause of drowning.

I remember one day at Bayville, Long Island, I met with a case of this sort, which only by good luck failed to end fatally. I was playing about the beach when I noticed a merry party of young men singing and frolicking on the raft which was anchored off shore. It was low tide when they went out, but the tide was coming in, and while they were still there the water became deep.

After a while they all came in with the exception of one young man who remained on the raft. I paid no attention to him, though I noticed that occasionally one of his companions would swim out to him and talk with him, and then return to shore. I wondered a little, but decided that there had been a quarrel and that he was staying out there for reasons of his own.

After a while, however, some of the young men came to me and asked me to go out and bring their companion in. They thought I was a guard stationed there to rescue drowning people.

"What is the matter with him?" I asked in surprise; 'why doesn't he come in himself? If he got out there I should think he could come back again."

"It was low tide then," they answered, "and it was easy to get out; now it is deep, and he's scared."
(Continued on page 136)

43/ FROM GREEK GOD TO 'PERFECTLY DEVELOPED'

Building the Physique of a "Greek God"

(Continued from page 41)

"Why don't you bring him in?" I persisted. "You can all swim."

"Yes," they answered, "we can swim and we could get him in all right, but he's so scared he won't come with us."

"Why should he come with me?" I demanded. "If he won't come with you, why should he come with a stranger?"

"Oh, you're big and strong, and he might trust you. And something must be done or he'll freeze to death. He's all blue now."

I realized then that it was growing cool. It was late in the season and the afternoons were cold, though it was only delightful when one was exercising. It seemed odd to me, however, that any one would sit out there alone on the raft and turn blue with cold rather than let his friends help him ashore to comfort and safety.

"All right," I said, "I'll go out and bring him in."

I'm not a specially fine swimmer, but I'm a good, strong one; and I had practiced rescue work so that I had no doubt of my ability to bring the man in. I swam out to him. He sat there on the raft, washed by the waves as they broke over it. He was blue with cold and his teeth chattered; but his trouble was fear. His eyes were wide and staring, and he was all huddled up.

"I'll take you ashore," I said. "Come to the edge of the raft."

Not he. He refused in a panic-stricken voice to budge an inch. I assured him I could get him back in safety; and told him he would perish if he remained there. But nothing I could say made any difference to him; he was convinced he would drown if he got off the raft.

"Get a boat! get a boat!" he kept repeating.

"But I don't know where to find a boat," I said.

"Then I'll stay here," he moaned; "I'll drown if I go in the water; I know I will."

I never saw such a fellow, though I've heard of similar cases since then. He would actually rather sit there and probably die of fright and cold than take a chance in the water. I have been told that the best thing for me to have done was to stun him with a quick blow and then take him ashore; but it didn't occur to me to try any such heroic treatment. I didn't know where to find a boat, but I swam ashore and hunted until I found one. I had to put him in the boat, he was so numbed.

Fear is a shocking thing to see in another person under any circumstances, but I don't think I ever saw anything so abject as that man as he sat on the raft. It doesn't seem so bad when a girl is frightened, for we rather expect them to be timid; and yet I don't believe girls would be the timid creatures they are if they learned to be more self reliant by developing themselves physically.

Of course a great many girls nowadays are learning the delight of physical strength, and are finding out that they can be even more attractive when they are strong and independent; but there are too many who seem to think that their weakness is a drawing card until they come to grief through it.

One night as I was going to take the subway at the Flatbush Avenue station in Brooklyn, after having been to the Y. M. C. A. gymnasium, I saw a number of young men surrounding a girl and teasing her. I supposed they were friends of hers and was passing by without paying any attention to them, when I heard something she said that indicated to me that she was being annoyed.

I suppose being a family man—I have a beautiful wife and two lovely children—makes me more sensitive to that sort of thing. Anyhow I pushed my way through the men.

"Are they annoying you, Miss?" I asked. "Do you know them?"

She answered tearfully that she didn't know them and that they were annoying her and wouldn't let her go to the station.

"Come with me!" I said, taking her by the arm, "I'll see that you get to the station."

They crowded about me and began to threaten me, but I pushed them aside and told them to be careful if they didn't want to be hurt. When they saw I wasn't afraid of them and realized that I must be pretty strong to throw them aside so easily, they let me pass, but at the same time assured me that they would "get me" for interfering with them.

I took the girl to the station and then went back to where the rowdies stood. "Here I am," I said, "if you want to get me. But curs like you wouldn't try to get a man; weak girls are your game."

They backed away and swore at me; and one of them cried out, "We'll get you yet."

"Any time you like," I answered. "You'll find me here most every night about this time. I'll be looking for you to get me."

Of course I never heard from them again. That sort of fellow is always looking for easy game. It was quite enough for them that I showed I wasn't afraid of them. I don't believe they would have bothered the girl if she hadn't been afraid.

I don't think of anything else to say, and I don't imagine I have said this much very well, not being used to putting my ideas on paper; but I do hope that in some way I have said something that will help anyone who reads this. Even my simple story will have been worth while if it starts some ambitious young men on the road to physical strength and beauty.

04 'PERFECTLY DEVELOPED'

After winning the 1922 title, MacFadden offered Charlie either $1,000 in Prize money, or the lead role in the forthcoming Hollywood movie, *The Adventures of Tarzan*. Although Atlas was keen to showcase his famous physique in a major movie, his mother and wife were unhappy with the idea as Hollywood had a scandalous reputation in the 1920s. So Charlie took the money and remained in Brooklyn. The movie role returned to actor, Elmo Lincoln (above), who starred in the original 1918 movie, *Tarzan of the Apes*. After the silent motion picture era ended, Lincoln left acting to try his hand at mining.

45/ FROM GREEK GOD TO 'PERFECTLY DEVELOPED'

04 'PERFECTLY DEVELOPED'

(Above) The Physical Culture Magazine and its publisher, the eccentric Bernarr MacFadden (1868-1955). (Below) MacFadden's Physical Culture Hotel in Dansville, New York, once popular with celebrities and movie stars, was closed in 1971 and has been left derelict since.

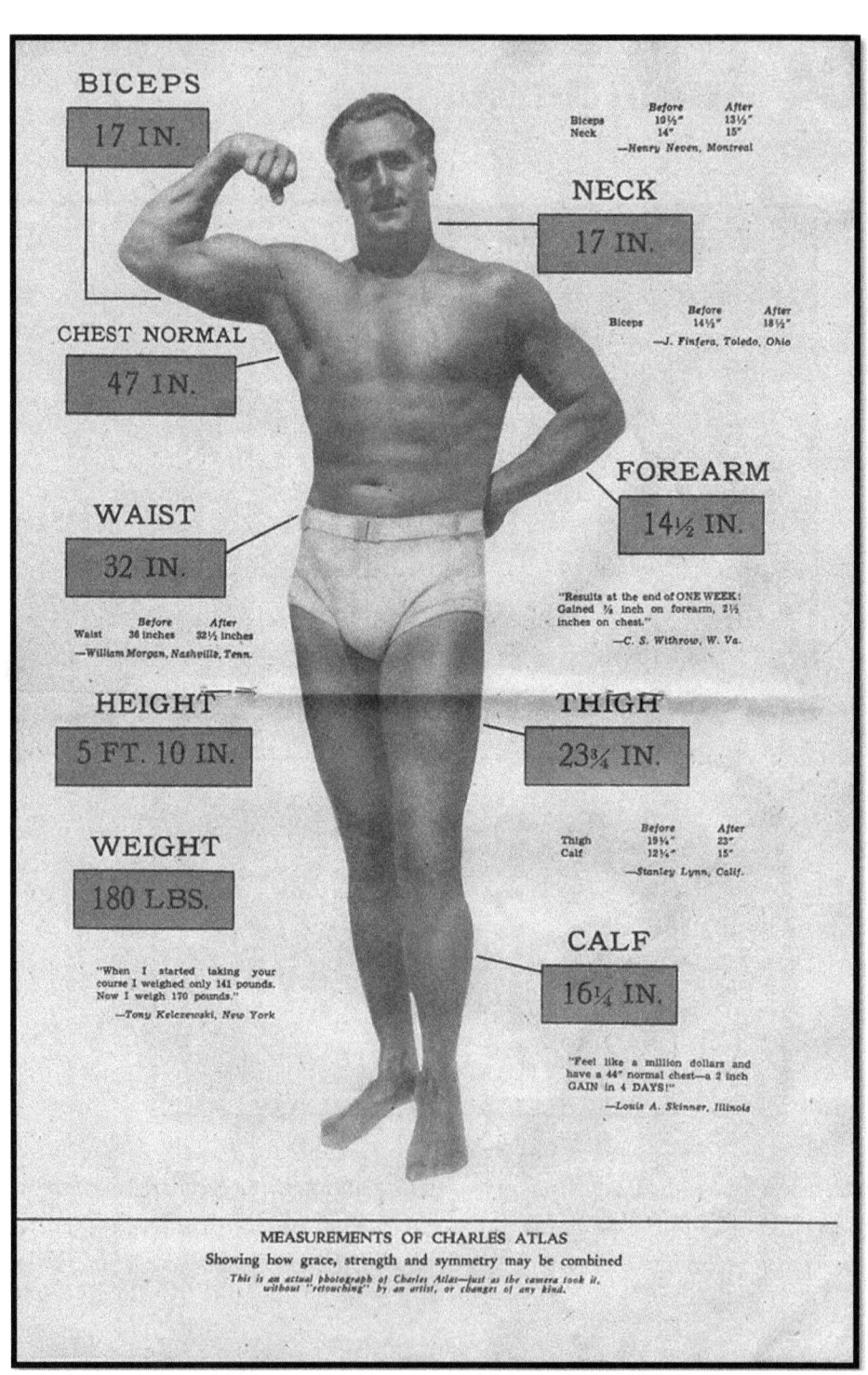

The center page from an Atlas brochure, displaying his measurements.

05 MAIL ORDER MUSCLES

It was time for Charlie to move on and find a way to capitalize on his fame, but he wasn't entirely sure which road to follow. He was young, handsome, becoming increasingly famous, and had the world in the palm of his hand. But what should his next move be?

In 1922, Bernarr MacFadden had decided to market a short film entitled *'The Road to health.'* He chose Charles Atlas to star as the fitness model, but later shelved the idea as he felt that the production would give Atlas too much publicity. However, just as Atlas was pondering his next move, another development suddenly presented itself to him, almost out of the blue.

The director of the film was Dr. Frederick Tilney, a homeopathic physician from Norwich on the east coast of England. Tilney and his wife immigrated to the USA in 1920 and worked for a time for the Winchester Rifle Company. Tilney entered and won a writing contest sponsored by the Waterman Pen Company, and was later hired by Bernarr MacFadden as a professional course writer his "ideas man." Tilney, who was known as "Doc," was responsible for introducing Charlie to MacFadden, after seeing him demonstrate the spring exercisers in a vacant store window. It was an encounter that proved to be fortuitous for both men. Tilney and Atlas became firm friends, and the Doc could see great potential for them both in the world of health and fitness, which was still a fledgling industry at the time.

During the making of 'The Road to Health', Tilney recalls the following story in his biography *"Young At 73 and Beyond - How to keep eternally youthful and remain tireless, painless, ageless"* (Information Inc., 1968), he hit on the idea of marketing a mail order bodybuilding course with Atlas.

05 MAIL ORDER MUSCLES

Here's how "Doc" explained it in his book: *"Every day for months, he (Charles Atlas) and I would drive in a luxurious limousine to Universal Films at Fort Lee, New Jersey. And there we would shoot the films. The script, called* **"THE ROAD TO HEALTH"** *was written by Carl Easton Williams, managing editor of Physical Culture Magazine. Mr. Atlas was, and is, a "prince" of a fellow and we became fast friends. He did a superb, natural job of acting and we made a wonderful movie. There were many others in the cast, but Mr. Atlas' Herculean physique was so majestic and beautiful it overshadowed everything else.*

When the movie was finished, Mr. MacFadden, the cast and myself went to see it shown in a projection room. He loved publicity, and the only mention of him was on the title. It was a "silent" movie, as "talkies" were not invented until 1925. But Macfadden realized that this would give Mr. Atlas a million dollars' worth of free publicity. So, to get his investment back he sent the films over to England and throughout Europe; the movies were shown there and made it profitable without showing it in the United States. Later he gave the film to Mr. Atlas who kept it in the can for years. One time I asked him to show it: he went to open the can and found the film had disintegrated, crumbled to powder and useless. "It was while driving with Mr. Atlas back and forth to the studios I suggested that he and I start a mail order business. We did and our first ad appeared in November 1922. We were business associates for many years, and he has told me that the years spent in association with me were the happiest in his life."(Young At 73 And Beyond - How to keep eternally youthful and remain tireless, painless, ageless. Pages 303-304).

The course marketed by Doc and Atlas was a straight fifty-fifty product. Tilney wrote the health and dietary advice, while Atlas put together the exercise regime. Both men were very knowledgeable in these areas, and by focusing on one discipline each, they were able to put together a superb program entitled; 'Health & Strength, by Charles Atlas.' They ran the business out of Tilney's home for the first six months, and their first ad appeared in physical Culture magazine in November, 1922. They quickly made enough money to rent a decent office and expand the business.

05 MAIL ORDER MUSCLES

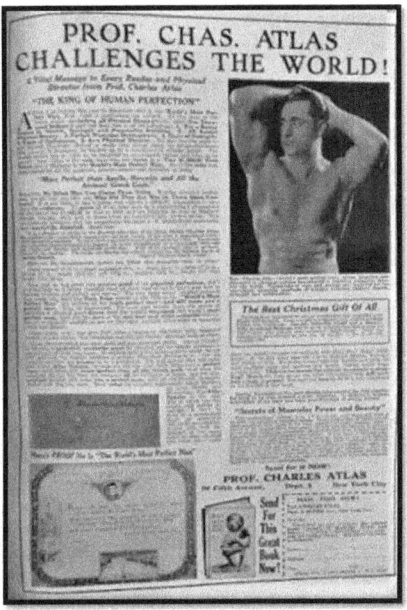

These early examples of Atlas' magazine advertising were the creations of Frederick "Doc" Tilney. As with many strongmen of the late nineteenth and early twentieth centuries. Atlas adopted the title of "Professor'" of physical culture, and was promoted by Tilney as the "king of human perfection".

'The advertisement on the right features two of Atlas' top students, including teenager Anthony Sansone, who later became known as the 'most beautiful man in America'. He was also a successful model, ballroom dancer, gym owner and a generous benefactor for underprivileged boys

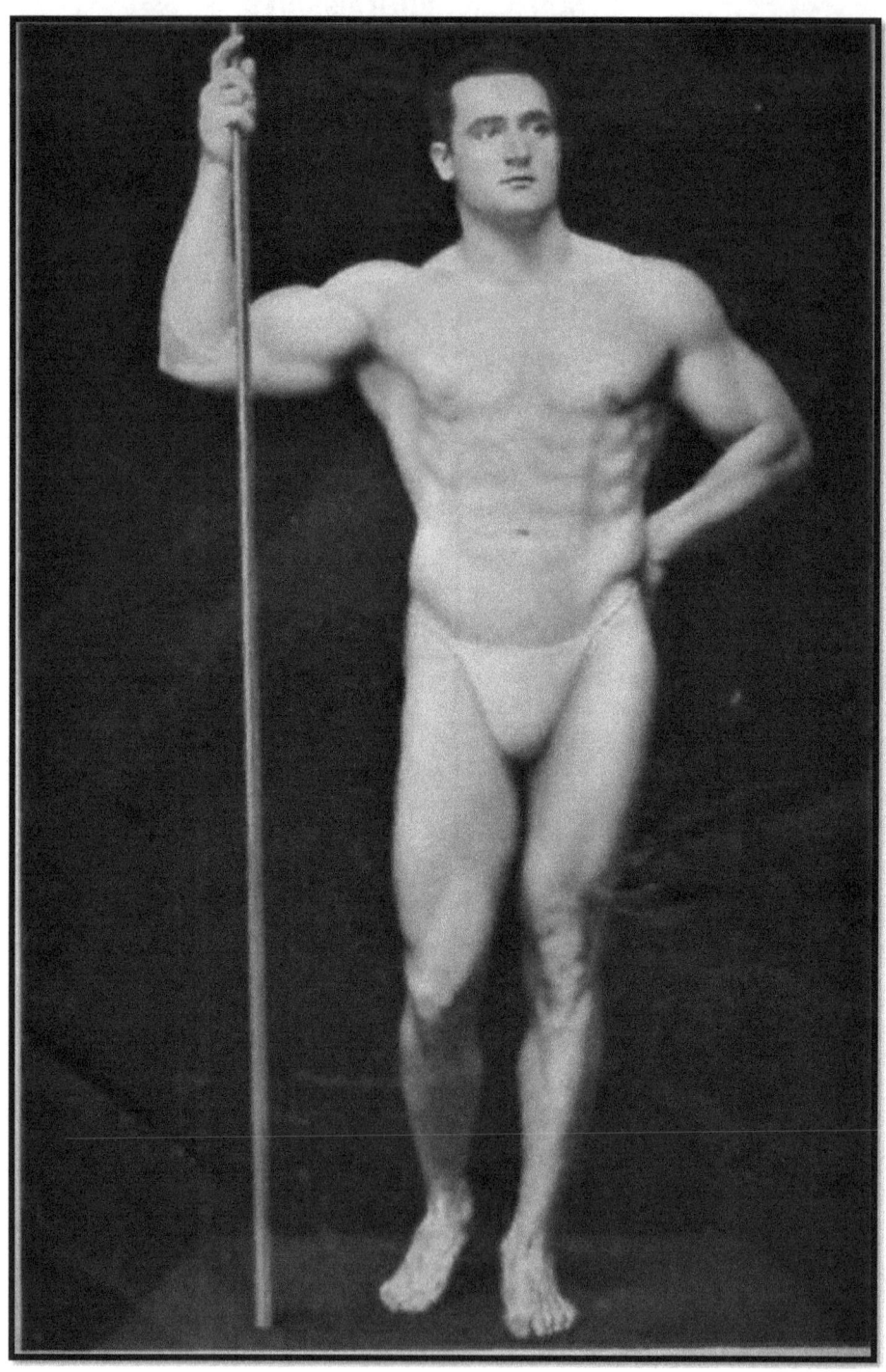

This photograph taken from Atlas' 1924 brochure, 'The Secrets of Health & Beauty,' highlights his perfectly proportioned physique. Few bodybuilders today would look as impressive in this pose

05 MAIL ORDER MUSCLES

Tilney and Atlas practiced what they preached. When the girls in the office all went out for lunch, the two men would change into their swimsuits and exercise for an hour in Atlas' private office. When the girls came back to the office, Tilney and Atlas would freshen up, dress, and head out for lunch.
On one occasion a man paid them a visit during their exercises regime:

"One day a man came bursting into Atlas' office.........stood there amazed, watching us exercise. He said, "How much is your course?" Mr. Atlas said, "thirty dollars," and went on exercising. The man said, "sign me up." He pulled a roll of bills out of his pocket, peeling off three tens, and laid them on the desk. So I signed him up. Mr. Atlas said, "as a rule, we have to give a sales talk before we enroll a student.

Would you mind telling us how you decided so quick?" The man said, "I just came over from Newark, calling on a competitor of yours. I had previously sent for his catalog, where he showed one photo of himself, and in his booklet he condemned smoking. I went to his office and had to pay ten dollars for a private consultation. I noticed he was sucking on a big fat cigar, and he had a terrible paunch.

I got so disgusted, I walked out and came right over here. I burst into your office, and what do I find? Both you fellows really practicing what you preach......so you get my money. ("Young At 73 And Beyond - How to keep eternally youthful and remain tireless, painless, ageless." page 74)

05 MAIL ORDER MUSCLES

Frederick Tilney (1895-1977) was a giant in the early physical culture and bodybuilding industry as a course writer, fitness instructor and author. He established a mail order bodybuilding course with Charles Atlas from 1922 to 1928. He and Atlas remained firm friends after moving to Miami, Florida where he established a successful health food business.

05 MAIL ORDER MUSCLES

In 1924, the government of Bermuda invited Tilney and Atlas to the island to present lectures on health, and display Mr. Atlas' impressive physique with demonstrations of his considerable physical strength. Apart from Tilney's lectures, Atlas would tear two telephone books in half together, bend rail road spikes into perfect "U" shapes, and supported a 1.5 inch thick iron bar in his teeth while two men hung onto each end. During one such demonstration before a large audience, Atlas instructed Tilney to take off his shirt.
As Doc recalled in his book:

"Then I came out and stood under the spotlight, he knew I was in good condition, as we had been training together for more than two years. Then he said, "I'm going to punch Dr. Tilney in the stomach." I tensed my abdominal muscles while he continued to powerfully punch into my abdomen time and again with all the force of his mighty fist. It didn't phase me in the least. It was like punching into a rock.

The audience was aghast at this unexpected and sensational demonstration. He told the audience; "See, he has the strength where it's really needed. He has a powerful stomach. That means he will never be constipated, never suffer from any ulcers of the stomach, never have any digestive upsets, he won't be suffering from rupture or any other trouble with his abdomen."("Young At 73 And Beyond – How to keep eternally youthful and remain tireless, painless, ageless." page 212)

05 MAIL ORDER MUSCLES

Charles Atlas supporting a 1.5 inch steel bar with his teeth while two men hung on each end. His feats of strength amazed and thrilled an audience of 7,500 people, and won him many new students from Bermuda. This was one of many feats of strength that he performed in front of huge crowds through out his career.

55/ MAIL ORDER MUSCLES

Atlas on the cover of the May 1924 edition of Physical Culture magazine. His chest, arm and shoulder development were outstanding even by today's standards

05 MAIL ORDER MUSCLES

Tilney liked the climate in Bermuda and suggested to Atlas that they move the business to Florida or California and wanted to scout out some locations. Atlas replied "go ahead." Eventually, when Tilney decided on Miami, Florida, Atlas had purchased a new home, and his wife, Margaret, did not want to leave her family and friends behind in Brooklyn. So Atlas, and the business stayed put. Earle Liederman, who was by 1924 the king of the mail order bodybuilding business was selling a thousand body building courses a week by mail and employed 300 secretaries to sort out his mail. Liederman also predicted that Atlas would not remain in business for very long, which made Charlie all the more determined to prove him wrong. From 1925 to 1928, Atlas and Tilney soldiered on with his mail order business. Charlie also invested in a modest gymnasium, where he taught his exercise system to attending 'pupils,' while Tilney still dreamed of moving to Florida.

But running two businesses was beginning to stretch even Charles Atlas a little too thinly and he closed the gym in 1928 to focus on the mail order business. This was an era where numerous physical culturalists were in the business of order muscles, and the competition was fierce. Earle E. Liederman was selling a thousand courses a week and employed 300 Secretaries to sort out his mail. Lionel Strongfort, Alois P. Swoboda also marketed their popular bodybuilding courses, and Bernarr Macfadden's physical culture empire was still going strong. The man who started the modern exercise movement, Eugen Sandow, died in 1925 at the age of 58, apparently from a stroke after lifting his car from a ditch.

However, it was suspected that Sandow actually died from complications arising from untreated syphilis that he acquired during an extra-marital affair. His wife, Blanche, buried him in an unmarked grave, which remained uncared for and overgrown until 2008, when his great-great-grandson, Chris Davies, installed a one-and-a-half ton pink sandstone monument at the grave.

57/ MAIL ORDER MUSCLES

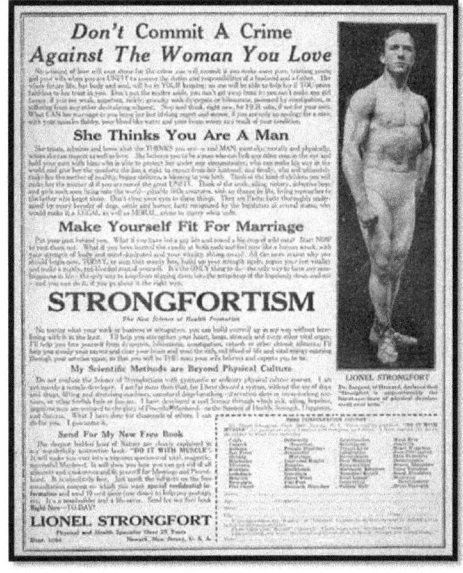

(Top left) Earle E. Liederman (Top right) Alois P. Swoboda, (Bottom left) George F. Jowett (Bottom right) Lionel Strongfort

05 MAIL ORDER MUSCLES

In Great Britain, several mail order bodybuilding course were being marketed, including the highly successful 'Maxalding,' a system of muscular development that relied upon a combination of muscle control movements, body-weight exercises and light dumbbell work. The course had been on the market since 1904, and was developed by the powerfully built, but unfortunately named Austrian strongman, Max Sick, with his English partner, Monte Saldow.
The course was still being marketed by Monte's son, Courtland Saldo, until his death from a heart attack in 1983 at the age of 73.

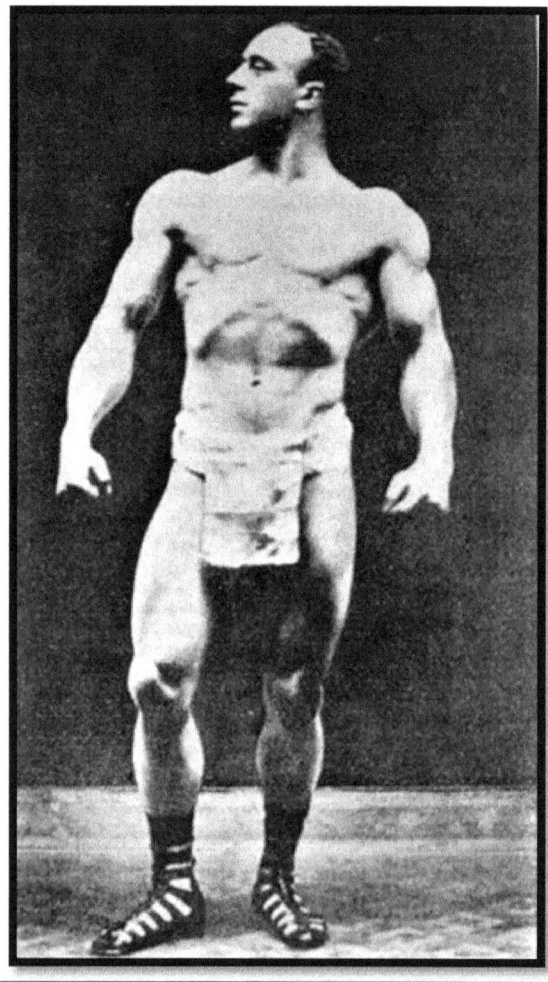

05 MAIL ORDER MUSCLES

The first course marketed by Charles Atlas was unique in that it did not require any equipment to secure good results. Other mail order muscle men sold apparatus to complement their course, such as small dumbbells sets or spring exercisers. None of the exercises in Atlas' course were particularly new, but he invented at least seven of them, and the entire exercise regime was cleverly blended to produce powerful results in the shortest possible time.
The health and dietary advice, written by Tilney were cutting edge at that time – and worked.

In September 1928, Atlas approached the Benjamin Lansdown Advertising Agency, to help out with the marketing of his course. His account, which was apparently the least profitable they had, was passed over to Charles P. Roman, a 22-year-old graduate from New York University. It was a meeting that was to spark a world-wide revolution in the fledgling world of bodybuilding.

Roman immediately saw the vast potential that Atlas and his course had, and immediately went to work. He started by changing the somewhat ineffective magazine ads that were originally written by Tilney. Roman knew that to promote the Atlas course to a larger market, he would have to promote Atlas. New, more eye-catching ads appeared *in Physical Culture, Popular Mechanics, The Ring, Family Circle, Health & Strength,* and a variety of boys' comic books and magazines.
The ads had unforgettable slogans such as;

> "You too, can have a body like mine!"

05 MAIL ORDER MUSCLES

Perhaps the most memorable was, "How I made a Man out of Mack," about a skinny youth who loses his girl after a bully kicks sand in his face. Mack, who is "sick and tired of being a scarecrow," sends off for the Charles Atlas course. After a few months, a more muscular Mack returns to the beach and decks the bully with a well-aimed right hook. He also wins back his girl, along with the admiration of her friends on the beach. The ads were a hit with thousands of men and boys, all over the world and Atlas started receiving more mail overnight that he had seen in years along with vastly improved sales.
He *knew* that he had found the right man to take the company to new heights.

Growing weary of the snowy New York winters, Doc Tilney knew that it was time to move on. After discussing his plans with Atlas to move to Miami, Atlas offered Charles Roman a partnership in his company.
Roman accepted and bought out Tilney for $500. Soon after Doc and his wife moved to Florida, where they ran a very successful health food business for many years.

Roman quickly got to work and edited Atlas' *Health & Strength* course to his satisfaction. He also renamed the system, "*Dynamic Tension*," and added photos of Atlas performing the exercises, as the earlier version of the program was not illustrated. The modest business that Tilney and Atlas started in 1922 was quickly taken to new and exciting heights by the genius of Charles P. Roman. Earle Liederman, who had established himself as the king of mail order muscles at that time, assured the two men that they would be out of business within six months.

05 MAIL ORDER MUSCLES

Eight months after Charles Atlas Ltd began operating, the stock market crashed on 'black Tuesday,' October 29, 1929. However, sales of the course flourished, and within a year, Roman purchased a drop head Rolls Royce. By 1930, he bought himself a boat and joined the Hudson River Yacht Club. Atlas, on the other hand, was more frugal, putting his money away and helping out family members who had fallen on hard times.

As Charles Atlas Ltd continued to grow, Earle Liederman began to see his own sales dwindle. Unlike Atlas, who was by all accounts a modest man, Liederman loved to show off. Apart from the 300 secretaries he employed in his swank New York offices, He spent a small fortune advertising his mail order body building course in a variety of newspapers and magazines. Liederman and his wife Helmar, a former Miss Alaska, moved around in high society circles while living in a $3,000 per month suite at the Plaza Hotel.

As the Great Depression worsened, most young men that were the backbone of Liederman's customer base no longer had the money to purchase his course, priced at $19.00. Helmar decided that she was unwilling to stick around in harder times and eventually left Liederman. According to divorce records filed in West Palm Beach County, Florida, Helmar moved away from Earle in the fall of 1930, and eventually divorced him in 1932.

Liederman's misfortunes worsened in May 1931 when, the Federal Trade Commission and local Better Businesses Bureau, investigated Liederman's muscle building enterprise, including his outlandish claims to turn thin young men into modern-day Eugene Sandows. On January 6, 1932, the New York Times reported that Liederman had filed for bankruptcy, showing that he had assets of only $2,500. At the peak of his bodybuilding empire, Liederman generated sales of nearly $1,000,000 a year. His fall from prince to pauper was dramatic and very public.

05 MAIL ORDER MUSCLES

However this was not the end for Liederman, who had the knack of landing on his feet. He reinvented himself as the "Wandering Poet" on the CBS radio network, hosting an exercise show for a largely female audience, ending each broadcast by reading his own rather sappy poetry on the air. On the advice of a former student, Liederman later moved to California in the 1940s, where he worked for bodybuilding guru, Joe Weider, as an editor for Muscle Power and Your Physique magazines. And it was Liederman who inspired a new generation of bodybuilders to move to California, where the legendary 'muscle beach' was established at Santa Monica. He died in 1970 at the age of 86, the victim of an auto accident.

63/MAIL ORDER MUSCLES

Earle and Helmar Liederman. The former Miss Alaska left him after the collapse of his body building empire in 1930, eventually divorcing him in 1932. Earle later moved to California where he worked as a magazine editor for Joe Weider

05 MAIL ORDER MUSCLES

The main reason why the Atlas-Roman partnership worked was because Atlas was simply the real deal, a genuine and caring man who was passionate about helping others. This was evident in the *Dynamic Tension* course, which was not just about developing better health and strength. The course contained valuable advice on the care of hair, teeth and skin. Personal grooming and developing a "magnetic personality" were all part of the package. Indeed, Atlas was ahead of his time in this regard, promoting the virtues and benefits of powerful positive thinking, years before the publication of Dale Carnegies' influential book, '*How to Win Friends and Influence People*' (Simon & Shuster, 1936).

Atlas not only advertised himself as 'the world's strongest physical director,' he proved it by performing a series of jaw dropping feats of strength throughout the 1920s and 1930s. He could tear two telephone books in half faster than any other man alive, and regularly bent *two* six-inch rail road spikes in half together.

Perhaps the two most challenging feats of strength performed by Atlas were the ones that really demonstrated his capabilities and won him wide public acclaim. In 1924 at the age of 32, Atlas pulled six cars a full mile with his neck. Then in 1938 at the age of 46, he pulled a 72 ton Pennsylvania rail road car along a level track for 112 feet at the Sunnyside Rail yard on Long Island.

He would regularly bend six inch nails into a 'U' shape and give them away to admiring members of the public as souvenirs. These were outstanding feats of strength for a man who never weighed more than 180lbs at his peak. Atlas once pressed 266 lbs above his head in a one arm bent-press movement, one of the heaviest lifts ever achieved by any strength athlete of comparable body-weight.

05 MAIL ORDER MUSCLES

On several occasions, Charlie was offered large sums of money from men who wanted him to sire "perfectly developed" children with their wives, but the strongman stated that he could never betray his wife, Margaret for any amount of money!

05 MAIL ORDER MUSCLES

Joseph (Joe) Bonomo (1901 – 1977) advertised himself as 'The World's Perfect Strongman,' perhaps still a little miffed at losing out on a major contest to his pal, Charles Atlas! After his movie career, Joe became a successful entrepreneur, and marketed a number of health and fitness booklets that can still be found today on Ebay.

67/MAIL ORDER MUSCLES

(Above) Joe lifting 200lb wrestler, Al Baffert above his head with one arm. His popularity as a strongman and trainer made him a legend in the fledging world of bodybuilding.

06 ATLAS VS HOFFMAN

In 1932, Charles Atlas Ltd came under the spotlight of the Federal Trade Commission. The main antagonist was Bob Hoffman, who made his living by selling oil burners before founding the York Barbell Company in 1932. Hoffman publicly called Charles Atlas 'the world's greatest fakir,' and called his exercise system 'dynamic hooey' in the pages of his magazine, '*Strength & Health*.' Hoffman was adamant that absolutely no one, not even Charles Atlas, could develop a strong, muscular physique without lifting weights.

The case went to court, and Hoffman tried to impress everyone (specially the press) by bringing along a troupe of weightlifters as proof of the 'superiority' of weights over Atlas' non-apparatus methods. Hoffman did a handstand on his thumbs while Atlas took his shirt off and demonstrated how the *Dynamic Tension* system actually worked. In truth, all Atlas had to do was to take several of his students down to the court with him to prove what his system could really do, as his filing cabinets were bulging with photos and testimonial letters from students all over the world, delighted with the results that *Dynamic Tension* training had given them.

Hoffman, most likely brought the case against Atlas out of nothing more than professional jealousy. Hoffman sold expensive sets of weights, while Atlas sold a mail order course that did not require equipment of any kind. The courts decided in Atlas' favor and a gag order was placed against Hoffman to cease and desist from making disparaging remarks about Atlas and his course in public.

06 ATLAS VS HOFFMAN

In 1937, Atlas again under scrutiny, but this time for some of his advertising claims. The one ad that caught the eye of the FTC was *"Let Me Prove In Seven Days, I can Make You A Man!"* In this case, Atlas proved that if you followed the principle exercise in his course – the chair dips – every morning and every night for seven days, you will see the results in your chest and arm muscles.

He was again given the all clear by the FTC, but was again cautioned about using certain wording in his ads. To be fair to Atlas, he did not actually write those ads himself, and other strongmen of the day made no less sensational claims for their own products, but were ignored by Hoffman whose jealousy of Atlas became an obsession.

FEDERAL TRADE COMMISSION FINDING OF FACT SAYS
CHARLES ATLAS IS TRUE TO HIS TEACHINGS

"This case involves the system of physical culture known as the Atlas Dynamic Tension system, developed and conducted by Mr. Charles Atlas. The Commission has previously found that Mr. Atlas "has employed and developed his said system since he was seventeen years of age and has attained his own great strength by the use of his own methods without relying upon apparatus" (Findings Paragraph Four, Docket No. 2542) " Again in Paragraph Four of its findings in Docket 2542, the Commission said:

"In other articles written by respondent (Hoffman) and by some of his employees, false, disparaging and defamatory statements are made, in that they refer to a competitor's system as 'dynamic hooey,' imply that no strength can be developed without the use of apparatus, that the use of dumbbells or barbells is absolutely essential to the development of strength and that no athlete can attain great strength without the use of apparatus.

06 ATLAS VS HOFFMAN

Among respondent's competitors is one Charles Atlas who has his principal place of business in New York City. Said Atlas likewise sells a course in physical training by mail in interstate commerce. He has developed a system of training in which he employs no apparatus whatever and which he has called '*Dynamic Tension*.' Said system is based entirely upon the resistance of one part of the body against another part. The records show that he has employed and developed his said system since he was seventeen years of age and has attained his own great strength by the use of his own methods without relying upon apparatus. Some years ago there was awarded to him in a competitive meeting of athletes in New York City the title of '**The World's Most Perfectly Developed Man**,' and he is widely known throughout the athletic world by that title."

A Gag order was then issued against Hoffman by the FTC not to disparage Atlas, or Atlas's company ever again. The FTC charged Hoffman, among other things, with unfair disparagement of its, competitor, Charles Atlas, Ltd.

The FTC Docket Numbers are 1952 (May 15, 1931 and the order for dismissal came in March 1932), 2542 (From 1936-1937 the Commission again considered the efficiency of the Atlas system of physical culture, this time collaterally, but nonetheless thoroughly and in a manner and with a result which entitled Charles Atlas, Ltd. to rely upon the finality of the Commission's judgment in Docket 1952) and 3308 case (Left) The FTC docket concerning advertising claims of Charles Atlas.

71/THE CHALLENGE: ATLAS VS HOFFMAN

(Left) Robert Collins (Bob) Hoffman, promoter of bodybuilding and weight lifting in 1932. (Right) Charles Atlas, promoter of physical development via his own non-apparatus *Dynamic Tension* system in 1930. It is clear to see how much more appealing, proportionate and aesthetic Atlas' physique is in comparison to his antagonist. The FTC case no doubt gave Atlas valuable publicity and most likely boosted the sales of his *Dynamic Tension* course.

72/THE CHALLENGE: ATLAS VS HOFFMAN

John C. Grimek (1910-1998) former U.S. Olympic heavyweight weightlifter and Mr. Universe winner. Grimek was an admirer of Charles Atlas and held him up as a "demi-god." Grimek always made a point of visiting Atlas in his New York office whenever he (Grimek) was in town.

06 ATLAS VS HOFFMAN

Perhaps as a sideswipe to Hoffman, Atlas wrote an article for the February 1936 edition of Physical Culture magazine called **'Every Man Every Day Should Do These.'** The article was accompanied by several photos of Atlas clad in his trademark leopard skin trunks demonstrating the exercises, looking trim and muscular at the age of 44. A year later, Atlas followed up with another article in the July 1937 edition of *Physical Culture* by writing another article called **'Are You Rich or Poor in Strength**?' posing again for the exercise photos.

One of Atlas' admirers was John C. Grimek, a weightlifter who competed in the 1936 Berlin Olympic Games and later progressed into bodybuilding. Grimek had been an admirer of Atlas for many years and held him up as a demi-god. During one of the FTC court hearings, Bob Hoffman took Grimek with him as part of his weightlifting team.

One afternoon during the proceedings, Grimek stepped out of the court room to take a drink from a water fountain and spotted Atlas leaving the court. Grimek shouted after Atlas, caught up with him, shook his hand and expressed his admiration for him. Atlas smiled, the two men chatted for a time, and thereafter became firm friends. Grimek went on to win two Mr. America titles and the 1948 Mr. Universe title in London England, defeating the magnificent Steve Reeves.

Grimek retired from competition undefeated, became editor in Chief of *Strength & Health* magazine, and remained in touch with Atlas. Visiting him on occasion at his New York office when he was in town. He later wrote about his regret at not stopping in to visit Atlas at his Palm Beach Florida home a few months before his passing on December 1972. It was a missed opportunity of a last meeting that Grimek deeply regretted. Atlas' old friend, Fred Tilney also felt badly, as he was contemplating writing Atlas' biography (at Atlas' request), but allowed other concerns to take up his time.

74/THE CHALLENGE: ATLAS VS HOFFMAN

> Actual photograph of Charles Atlas, "World's Most Perfectly-Developed Man", in the act of towing the 72½-ton car down the tracks of the Pennsylvania Railroad. (Photo by Acme).

Charles Atlas, pulling a 72.5 ton railcar along a lever track for 112 feet. He performed this feat of strength in 1938 at the age of 46. After completing this feat of strength, he pulled the car back to its original location, a total distance of 224 feet!

06 ATLAS VS HOFFMAN

Throughout the 1930s, Atlas was rarely out of the news. He appeared in news papers, magazines and as a frequent guest on radio talk shows. If you went to the movies, there was Charles Atlas in a news reel. He was photographed either performing feats of strength, judging a beauty show, or horsing around with famous athletes and celebrities of the day. By 1938, Atlas was wealthy, world-famous, happy and very content.

One of the things that set Atlas apart from other celebrities of the day was his squeaky clean image. He would regularly advise young boys to "live clean, think clean, and don't go to Burlesque shows." He strongly advised against smoking, drinking, and eating white sugar products.
The Mafia weren't slow to remember Atlas' Italian heritage. During a visit to Chicago, Al Capone sent a crate of champagne to Atlas' hotel room with an invitation to dinner. Atlas pretended to have a heavy chill and avoided the meeting with the gangster. On another occasion, a Mafia 'heavy' arrived at Atlas' office in New York and offered the strongman a Mafia credit card, but Atlas refused to accept it. When the goon tried to put it in Atlas' pocket, Charlie thumped the oaf and threw him out of his office.

By 1940, Atlas' *Dynamic Tension* system was a world-wide success, with sales at over 500,000 courses a year, and with two international offices, one in London and the other in Buenos Aires to handle overseas sales. The Dynamic Tension course was so successful it was printed in seven languages.
Life was good for the Atlas family. Charles Jr was now a handsome 20-year old with his sights set firmly on university, and daughter Diane, aged 19, was hoping to become a professional singer. Margaret Atlas kept the home, looking after her brood and cooking delicious Italian meals for family and friends. During the summer, the family would spend their days at their holiday home, a converted coast guard station on the beach at Point Lookout, Long Island. However, the dark shadow of war began to slowly loom over Europe, as Adolph Hitler, prepared to unleash hell.

76/THE CHALLENGE: ATLAS VS HOFFMAN

Above) Charles Atlas flexing his 17 inch bicep for world heavyweight boxing champion, Joe Louis. (Below) Doing push-ups with another world heavyweight boxing champion, Max Baer

07 ATLAS AT WAR

In 1938, for those living in Europe, the Orient and even the United States of America, it seemed that the world was beginning to come apart at the seams. The years leading up to the beginning of World War II were deeply troubling times for the world at large. The Great Depression had started ten years before, leaving much of the industrialized world desperate and struggling.
In the United States of America, production, profits, and wages had regained their 1929 levels, but unemployment was still high. Although it was slightly lower than the 25% rate of 1933. Within the mid-1937, throughout most of 1938, industrial production declined almost 30% and production of durable goods fell even faster.

It was not until 1941, when America entered World War II, did the economy begin to recover. Nationalism was sweeping through Germany, and the rise of the charismatic, but evil Adolph Hitler ensured the end of the Versailles Treaty that had imposed harsh conditions on Germany after the end of World War 1. The Empire of Japan sparked a war with China when they invaded Manchuria in 1931 and brutally slaughtered men, women and children, often burying them alive in mass graves. Germany, Italy, and Japan ignored the newly founded League of Nations that was unable to stop their invasions and occupations of nearby countries.

The Spanish Civil War broke out in 1936, and General Francisco Franco enjoyed the unwavering support of Adolph Hitler, who dispatched armored units and Luftwaffe squadrons to assist in the deposing of President Nacito Alcala-Zamora. The intervention gave Hitler's military forces valuable combat experience, but in order to prepare for World War II, the Fuhrer persuaded Mussolini of Italy to send in larger military units to ensure General Franco's success. On September 1st 1939, Hitler invaded Poland and unleashed the satanic evil of Nazi rain cloud onto Europe.

07 ATLAS AT WAR

America watched and reluctantly waited, during an economic depression to engage in another emerging world war that was primarily being fought in Europe. Massive amounts of military hardware poured into Britain, France, China, and the Soviet Union from the United States as part of a lend-lease agreement to provide food, oil, and other materials between 1941 and August 1945. This included warships and warplanes, along with other weaponry.
It was signed into law on March 11th 1941, and ended in September 1945.

79/ ATLAS AT WAR

The Atlas family at their summer home in Point Lookout, Long Island in 1938

07 ATLAS AT WAR

Charles Atlas continued to make publicity appearances. He bent and broke iron bars during a strength demonstration in front of 3,000 cheering prisoners at Sing Sing Prison, located at the town of Ossining, thirty miles north of New York City. Charles Roman telephoned the press and suggested the headline;

"Man breaks iron bars at Sing Sing, Prisoners cheer, no-one escapes"

Roman proved he was just as adept at arranging clever publicity appearances for Atlas, than he was developing those infamous magazine and comic book ads. He was photographed posing with actress Dorothy Wilson (left), who was chosen by the Model's League of New York as the 'most perfect model.' Atlas was filmed by a newsreel crew performing a friendly "tug-of-war' with the Rockettes, a dance troupe, on the garden rooftop of the Radio City building in New York. And later supported all four on a pole balanced on his shoulders; a combined weight of over four hundred pounds. In the warm weather, Atlas ran on the beach Island, and on one occasion, he ran 10 miles in one hour, barefoot, along the country roads near his summer home at Point lookout, proving that he was as fit as he was strong.

One of the exercises prescribed in lesson one of the *Dynamic Tension* course, stressed the importance of full, deep breathing. This practice, along with the persistence of the chair dips, were a potent combination for developing a powerful set of lungs, a strong heart, and the stamina of a top athlete.

81/ ATLAS AT WAR

(Top) Charles Atlas engaged in a friendly tug-of-war with all six of the Rockettes. (Bottom) lifting four of the dancing troupe, a combined weight of over 400 pounds

07 ATLAS AT WAR

On April 30th 1939, the New York World's Fair opened and was located in Flushing Meadows Queens. The main purpose of the fair was to lift the spirits of the United States and generate much-needed business for New York City. The fair was also a cultural and historical affair, designed to correspond with the 150th anniversary of George Washington's first inauguration as President of the United States. On July 3rd, 1940, the fair hosted Superman Day to honor the legendary American comic book hero. Actor Ray Middleton made an appearance dressed as the 'man of steel,' but looked like he urgently needed to take the *Dynamic Tension* course.

However, the less than husky actor had a successful stage career, appearing in the Broadway hits *South Pacific, Annie Get Your Gun*, and others. During the world fair, a contest was held to find a 'super girl' and a 'super boy.' One of the judges for the contest was Charles Atlas. Eleven year old Maureen Reynolds from Manhattan and 15 year old William Aronis from Astoria Queens, were selected by Atlas. The panel included well-known personalities of that era such as Lucy Monroe, Ray Middleton, Frank Buck and Morris Gest. William Aronis was invited to visit Atlas at his office at 113 east 23rd Street, in New York. Although Aronis enjoyed his visit, he declined to buy the *Dynamic Tension* course.

83/ ATLAS AT WAR

Charles Atlas with Maureen Reynolds and William Aronis, 'Super Girl and Super Boy' winners at the New York World Fair in April, 1939.

07 ATLAS AT WAR

On July 4th at 4.45pm, the day after Charles Atlas appeared at the World Fair, a suitcase bomb containing dynamite, exploded at the British Pavilion, killing two New York police detectives, Joe Lynch and his long-time partner, Freddy Socha. Both men, who were attached to the Bomb & Forgery Squad, were instantly killed, and five civilians were injured. Although it was thought that the bomb had been planted by Nazi sympathizers, it could not be proven, Nevertheless terrorism had come to America, and the population of New York City were terrified.

Detectives Ferdinand (Freddie) Sochi (left) and Joseph (Joe) Lynch (Right) were killed when examining an explosive device at the New York World Fair on July 4th, 1939

07 ATLAS AT WAR

When the World Fair opened in April 1939, Germany had occupied two countries, Austria and Czechoslovakia. By time the fair ended in 1940, Belgium, Denmark, France and the Netherlands were all under Nazi control. Britain stood alone, and from July 10th to October 31st, the Royal Air Force fought continuously to stop the Luftwaffe from bombing the country into a surrender, thus preventing Operation Sea Lion, Hitler's planned invasion for the British Isles. During the war years, sales of the *Dynamic Tension* course were brisk, as young men realized their need to get into shape – fast! One particular promotional Atlas flyer stated;

"Yes – from **HEAD** to **FOOT** let me give you a **NEW BODY** that will help you fight the battles of life …..In **WAR** or **PEACE!**"

"SUPPOSE YOUR BODY IS CALLED TO DEFEND AMERICA". The duties in the services will be a "cinch" if you've got a strong, sturdy body that can "take it." Let me show you how to build up your own "national defenses" the proven *"Dynamic Tension"* way – as hundreds of soldiers, sailors, and marines are doing right now!

On March 11th 1941, President Franklin D. Roosevelt signed the Lend-Lease agreement, under which the United States of America provided thousands of tons of war materials to Great Britain. As well as the USSR, Republic of China, Free-France and other allied nations in an effort to resist the progress being made by Germany and the Empire of Japan in the rapidly escalating global war.

Although the United States did not want to commit its armed forces to engage in the war, this changed overnight on the morning of December 11th 1941, 353 Imperial Japanese Naval aircraft attacked the US Naval base at Pearl Harbor, Hawaii. All eight U.S. Navy battleships were damaged, with four being sunk. All but one were later raised, and six of the eight battleships returned to service and saw action in World War Two. The Japanese also sank or damaged three cruisers, three destroyers, one anti-aircraft training ship, and one mine-layer. In all, 188 U.S. aircraft were destroyed and 2,402 Americans were killed in the attack.

07 ATLAS AT WAR

The entire nation was thrown into a state of shock, and President Roosevelt publicly declared war on the Empire of Japan the next day. Germany then declared war on the USA on December 11th, and the US reciprocated on December 12th. Charles Atlas Jr turned 23 years of age that same day.

A year before Pearl Harbor, and perhaps in anticipation of a possible involvement in World war II, the Roosevelt government enacted *The Selective Training and Service Act of 1940*, which was the first peacetime conscription in United States history. The Act required that men between the ages of 21 and 35 register with local draft boards. In 1941 men aged 18 to 45 were made subject to military service, and all men aged 18 to 65 were required to register. During the draft in 1941, so many young men were being declared as medically unfit for military service, Charles Atlas publicly lost his cool and yelled at reporters:

"Why in the hell didn't the United States government do something about this, years ago? Why do we have to wait for an emergency to worry about the health of our young men?"

So the United States Government, whether out of embarrassment, necessity, or both, hired Atlas, who toured naval and army bases to demonstrate his *Dynamic Tension* training. Atlas was 49 years old in 1941, too old to be drafted. But he did dedicate the war years to ensuring that the officers and enlisted men in the U.S. military were fit to fight and fighting fit. Once again, Atlas found himself in the right place at the right time to help his nation fight the most horrific war in human history – and win it!

88/ ATLAS AT WAR

07 ATLAS AT WAR

By 1942, thousands of officers and enlisted men in all three branches of the United States military were being trained by Atlas to get them fighting fit and fit to fight. Charles Atlas Junior and Charles Roman both joined the U.S. Navy. Atlas served throughout the war as an ensign (a junior commissioned officer) and his ship took part in the D-Day invasion of Normandy on June 6th, 1944.

Roman served in the U.S. Coast Guard, keen to do his duty. He was also an officer and served in the Atlantic Theatre, protecting allied supply ships from marauding German submarines. He was directly involved in sinking three enemy submarines before his naval service ended with the war in 1945.

Charles Jr, also returned safely to his family. America and the Atlas family, had done their bit. The war was won, and many thousands of young men returned home alive. Thanks to the health, strength, fitness and motivation for victory they received through the joint efforts of the United States government and Charles Atlas.

08 POST WAR MUSCLES

From the 1950s onwards, the world was rapidly changing, and serious body building contests were springing up in the USA, Canada, and Great Britain. Atlas arrived in the USA in 1903, just one year after the Wright Brothers flew the first heavier-than-air machine. He witnessed the development of the life saving anti-biotic, penicillin in 1942, the atomic bomb in 1945, and the first communication satellite, Sputnik in 1957. He went from listening to music on a tall Victrola phonographic record player to a transistor radio in his kitchen and a color television in his front room. Throughout the 1950s, the new medium of television allowed Charles Atlas Ltd to air commercials for the *Dynamic Tension* course in Great Britain.

Over 500 newspapers, magazines and comic books carried ads for his course, using photos of Atlas that had been taken decades before. However, a TV news interview in 1961 revealed a shirtless Charles Atlas still muscular and virile at the age of 69. The company even sold sun tan lamps, encyclopedia sets, and even digital watches. He also started his own line of protein powder, vitamins and other health supplements. As the 1960s rolled on, almost all of Atlas' rivals in the mail order muscle business had gone, but a few exceptions still hung on. The man who was probably Atlas' first student, Joe Bonomo, had retired as a movie stuntman and successfully marketed a series of health & fitness booklets on isometric-isotonic training, barbell training, spring exerciser training, even beauty tips for women.

Bonomo even ran Atlas-style ads to sell his course, and once had a nationwide '*Bonomo Boys Health Club*,' which was endorsed by boxer Jack Dempsey.
The promoters of weight lifting, such as Joe Weider, Dan Lurie, Bob Hoffman, and the Scottish bodybuilder, Don Dorans, all sold booklets and courses that relied on training with weights to gain results. A few non-apparatus courses appeared over the years, such as the "*Dynaflex*" course, advertised in comic books by a muscular individual who rejoiced in the name of Mike Marvel.

91/ POST WAR MUSCLES

Magazine ads for mail order bodybuilding course from the 1960s and 1970s.

08 POST WAR MUSCLES

None of them had the endurance or appeal of Charles Atlas. The unlikely named "Saul New York" (above left) and his title "Mr. Perfect Physique" did not exist, as the head of a male model was placed on the body of 1967 Mr. America Don Howarth! However, Morrie Mitchell (Top right) was a real titled bodybuilder and personal trainer. (Below) The famous Charles Atlas magazine ad that encouraged millions of boys and men to enroll in the *Dynamic Tension* course and lead stronger, healthier and more productive lives.

93/ POST WAR MUSCLES

Charles Atlas aged 63, lifting model and actress Jo Anderson above his head with one arm

08 POST WAR MUSCLES

On April 17th 1965, Margaret Atlas died. She was diagnosed with a cancerous tumor, but did not survive the operation. Charles and Margaret Atlas had been devoted to each other since the day they met in 1918. Her tragic death sent Atlas spiraling into a deep depression. Margaret had always been there for him, and they were rarely apart. Atlas always came home to Margaret who greeted him with the same loving warmth in 1965 as she did when they first married 47 years before. Suddenly their Brooklyn apartment was filled with the sound of silence. His daughter, Diane Spinelli lived close by and supported him as best she could through the next year or so, which were probably the most lonely and desperate in Atlas' life. The thought of facing his remaining years alone were almost too much to bear. Atlas considered moving into a monastery to withdraw from the world so he could study, meditate and teach the Brothers healthy living habits and exercise routines. After several long conversations with his parish priest, he was talked out of the idea. Charles realized that the sparse life of a Benedictine monk was not his calling in life.

Atlas was where he needed to be. He was Charles Atlas, the World's Most perfectly Developed Man, an icon, a living trademark, and a hero to millions of boys and men all over the world. There wasn't a man in the world his age that looked like him or could inspire people like him. For a time he just wanted to disappear, but the world still needed Charles Atlas. By 1967, Charles Roman was under pressure from newspaper reporters and television stations. Where was Atlas? Had he died? Was he ill? How does he look today? Ridiculous rumors had spread like wildfire about Atlas during his absence. He was in a wheelchair, or his neck muscles got too big and choked him, or that he was suffering from a bone disease that had left him invalided. To dispel the rumors and take the pressure off Roman, Atlas decided to pose for a new set of publicity photos.

08 POST WAR MUSCLES

However, Roman didn't like the idea, believing that the photos of Atlas as he appeared decades ago were just fine.

"To whiten his hair would not be meaningful," Roman once told journalist, Philip Norman.

In the end, Roman agreed and Atlas posed for a new set of publicity photos, looking little different from his earlier years. He need not have worried. Atlas posed on the beach looking sensationally fit and tanned. His physical measurements had barely changed since the 1930's, and he still exercised every day, proving that *Dynamic Tension* could keep a man looking his best even into old age. In 1968 at the age of 77, Atlas appeared in a new magazine ad with two young bikini models, feeling his flexed 17 inch biceps. He bought a condo in Palm Beach Florida which he shared with Anne Lucas, his live in housekeeper and companion whom he met through his daughter.

He even went back to work, spending every afternoon answering mail and receiving visitors. The *Sunday Times* color supplement sent journalist Philip Norman and photographer Diane Arbus to visit Atlas at his Florida condo for an interview. Atlas was in high spirits, preaching his message of health and vitality, revealing an amazing memory for details and names. He still ate well, slept like a top, exercised daily and swam at the salt water pool at South Ocean Boulevard.

On another occasion Atlas was invited to an engagement party. Three elderly widows grabbed him and took him upstairs, proclaiming *"boy what we could do with you!"* Atlas thought that they were going to show him a work of art or a picture, until they made their real intentions clear. "Ladies," pleaded Atlas, *"I am seventy six years old!"*

08 POST WAR MUSCLES

He was regularly invited to parties by the Miami Mafia that he never attended, but one colorful mobster visited Atlas at his condo. "This guy drove over to meet me. I thought he was a movie star. Soft hat, thirty dollar shirt, and two guns he had," recalled Atlas. *(Sunday Times Color Supplement, 1969)* Atlas' Palm Beach condo was treated like a mecca of muscledom by devoted students and fans the world over, who would often just show up at his door to meet him. On another occasion he was visited by Edwin Pope, the sports editor for the Miami Herald. To Pope, Atlas had been a hero for many years, and so he took the opportunity to visit Atlas for an interview. In a 1982 biography on Atlas, written by Charles Gaines, Pope was quoted as saying; "He appeared to be a lonely, frightened man. We talked for three hours and I am sure that if I had invited him, he would have gotten into the car with me for a drive back to my office in Miami." *Yours In Perfect manhood, Charles Atlas. Simon & Shuster, New York, 1982)*

97/ POST WAR MUSCLES

Charles Atlas aged 69 in 1961, promoting his new brand of protein powder, vitamin pills and other supplements for sale by mail to his legions of students world-wide

98/ POST WAR MUSCLES

Who else could pose like this, tanned, fit, trim and muscular at 77 years of age? It was this magazine ad in the July 1970 edition of Hot Rod magazine that inspired many older men to send for the Dynamic Tension course and get back into shape

99/POST WAR MUSCLES

Charles Atlas (top) and his old pal, Joe Bonomo (below) maintained busy Office hours late into their careers, answering fan mail and greeting visitors.

08 POST WAR MUSCLES

When the author of this book contacted Pope many years later concerning his meeting with Atlas, Pope stated that he did not recall Atlas being frightened, but rather, meeting with Charles Atlas was "one of the nicest things that ever happened to him." This seemed to be the general consensus among the vast majority of people who visited Atlas in his later years either out of admiration for him, or just to see if he was a real person. His telephone constantly rang, and Atlas was even happy to advise people on overcoming their various problems in life.

Joe Weider with Dr. & Mrs. Fred Tilney in Miami, Florida in 1965. Weider and his brother Ben, established the International Federation of Bodybuilders (IFBB). They also sold magazines, food supplements, weights, and established the Mr. Olympia bodybuilding contest

101/ EVOLUTION OF A STRONGMAN

Atlas aged 19 to 75 Still rock hard!

102/EVOLUTION OF A STRONGMAN

Atlas at 78 years of age in 1970

103/EVOLUTION OF A STRONGMAN

Atlas and his live in companion, Anne Lucas, photographed in 1971.

09 EVOLUTION OF A STRONGMAN

In 1970, Atlas sold his half of the business to Charles Roman, who was now 64 years of age. He stayed on as a consultant and still posed for publicity photos, claiming that over seven million people had enrolled in his *Dynamic Tension* course. The course was still selling for $30.00, the same price it had been in 1922. This volume of sales would have generated $210 million dollars, an impressive amount of money even by today's standards. Even with a 10% return rate for those who wanted their money refunded, a return of $189.00 million dollars by 1970 was still a vast amount of money, regardless of staff salaries, overhead costs and taxes paid out by Charles Atlas Ltd. Little wonder Atlas' rivals were jealous; this kind of individual success was still a comparative rarity even in America, especially in the mail order muscle business.

In the last few years of his life, Atlas was diagnosed with a mild form of diabetes, inherited from his mother's side. He was advised to adopt a high protein diet to offset the effects of the disease, and to start taking it easy. In type 2 diabetes, the pancreas makes insulin, but it is not produced in the amount the body needs and is ineffective as a result. Protein, particularly whey protein, impacts the pancreatic cells in a positive way, and helps to release more insulin. This in turn, helps regulate blood glucose levels, and helps to manage type 2 diabetes. Atlas began to consume more protein that he was used to, eventually resulting in his arteries becoming congested.

But telling Charles Atlas to stop exercising was like telling Gene Krupa to stop playing the drums. But the great man knew his limitations and modified his exercise regime, which included using a stationary exercise bicycle on his balcony, wall pushups and self-resistance exercises. In mid-1972, Atlas began experiencing persistent chest pains after exercising and went for medical tests. The results were not encouraging and his doctors confirmed the worst.

09 EVOLUTION OF A STRONGMAN

By late December 1972, Atlas experienced more chest pains that were so severe he had to be hospitalized at Long Island's Memorial Hospital. On the evening of December 24th 1972, Charles Atlas, the *World's Most perfectly Developed Man* and hero to millions of boys and men all over the world, gently slipped into eternity as he slept in his hospital bed. He and his beloved Margaret were finally reunited.
It was over.

10 THE ATLAS LEGACY

By 1972, bodybuilding contests and gyms had sprung up all over the world. Since the passing of Charles Atlas, Joe Weider was regarded as the new king of bodybuilding, but it could be argued that most of his top physique stars had risen to prominence by winning the original 'Mr. Universe' contest in London England. Organized and ran by the National Amateur Bodybuilding Association, otherwise known as NABBA.

Roman reported that in spite of the rapid growth of gyms and health clubs around the world, business for Charles Atlas Ltd was as brisk as ever, and the company continued to receive letters from students addressed to Mr. Atlas personally, even ten years after the strongman's passing.

Mr. Roman passed away in 1999 at the age of 92, after selling the company to intellectual property lawyer, Jeffrey C. Hogue.

107/ THE ATLAS LEGACY

Above; Relaxing at his summer home in Point Lookout, L.I. Picture 2: On the beach at Palm Beach, FL. (3) Enjoying the sunshine on his balcony at Palm Beach (4) Celebrating his 78TH birthday at home in Brooklyn., NY.

108/ THE ATLAS LEGACY

Throughout his life, Charles Atlas was always in demand for television and radio appearances, promotions and interviews. Here he was interviewed for a national television news channel outside his condominium home in Palm Beach Florida in 1971. His enduring fame and appeal as a bodybuilder and purveyor of health & fitness was only surpassed by others after his death in December 1972. He was a truly unique and larger than life personality that has remained without equal today.

~ THE END~

CPSIA information can be obtained
at www.ICGtesting.com
Printed in the USA
LVHW101342280221
680188LV00033B/433